Oliver Rackham beside the Helford River at Calamansack Wood
Photograph by Pamela Tompsett, September 2007

Published by Little Toller Books in 2019
Little Toller Books, Lower Dairy, Toller Fratrum, Dorset

Typeset in Garamond and Perpetua by Little Toller Books

Printed in India by Imprint Press

All papers used by Little Toller Books are natural, recyclable products made from wood
grown in sustainable, well-managed forests

A catalogue record for this book is available from the British Library

ISBN 978-1-908213-68-6

PUBLISHED WITH THE SUPPORT OF:

Woodland Trust
National Trust
Corpus Christi College, Cambridge
Susan Ranson
Chris D. Preston

The Ancient Woods of
THE HELFORD RIVER

OLIVER RACKHAM

Edited by David Morfitt

with contributions from
Paula Keen and Simon Leatherdale

LITTLE TOLLER

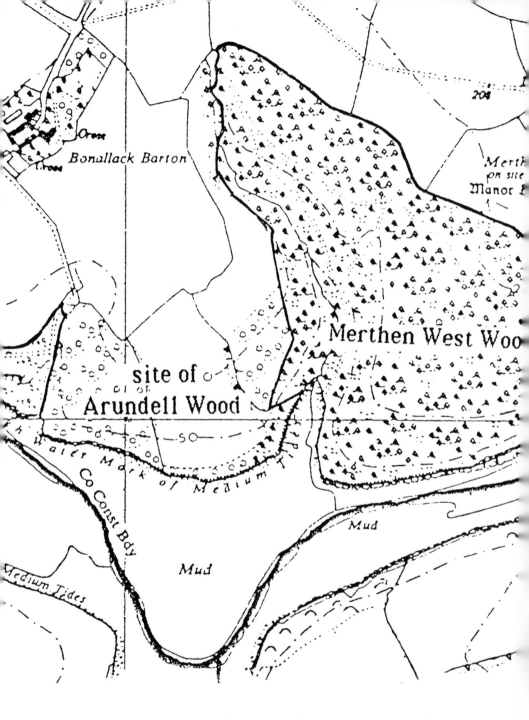

The detail above shows the site of Arundell Wood and Merthen Wood West; the thick line illustrates the limit of ancient woodland. This is one of many Ordnance Survey maps that Oliver Rackham carried and marked during his fieldwork. A selection of these Annotated Maps (AM) are referred to throughout the book and can be found from page 157.

Contents

PREFACE *by Oliver Rackham*   7

FOREWORD *by George Peterken*   9

EDITORIAL *by David Morfitt*   15

1   Introduction   21

2   Environment: geology and soils   28

3   History   32

4   Archaeology   61

5   Flora   68

6   Vegetation   78

7   Individual woods   102

8   Conservation   138

ANNOTATED MAPS   157

BIBLIOGRAPHY, NOTES AND REFERENCES   163

INDEX AND GLOSSARY   173

Preface

In its ecology, the Lizard Peninsula is an especially fascinating corner
of England; its landscape history is almost as marvellous. In 1966 Dr
D. E. Coombe, upholding a tradition of three hundred years among
Cambridge botanists, first introduced me to the Lizard. I well remember
our passage through the woods of Gweek and Treverry, a dramatic
initiation to this uniquely different land. The Helford River woods have
been less studied than the moors and cliffs of the Lizard, but I visited
them over the years and was delighted when in 1986 an opportunity
came to investigate them in detail. That study – commissioned by Kerrier
District Council with the support of the Countryside Commission –
was circulated privately but never published. However, I continued to
visit West Cornwall sporadically and revisited many of the woods in
2007. This expanded version is the product of these later studies; it is
no longer strictly confined to the Helford River.

My fieldwork would not have begun without the friendship and
enthusiasm of the late Dr Coombe, my teacher and lifelong colleague.
In the early years, I owed much to the company and discussion of
Mr S. Bott. Mr N. Davies arranged a boat trip and spent much time
explaining the excellent work of the National Trust. Dr H. J. B. Birks,
Dr A. Byfield, Dr J. Hopkins, Dr M. H. Martin, Dr C. Preston, M.
Schule, and the late Dr H. L. K. Whitehouse (most of them also
former students of Dr Coombe) have been with me in the field or have
supplied records. I have made use of a paper by Dr G. F. Peterken on
Calamansack Wood. On later visits I am most indebted to Dr Pamela
Tompsett of the Helford River Voluntary Marine Conservation Area,
and to Colin Hawke, Tree Officer of Cornwall County Council. I am
grateful to the private owners who allowed me to visit their woods.

This book was made possible by the collaboration of Oliver Padel, the Cornish language scholar, in his generous help with maps and documents, in discussion of linguistics and place-names, in fieldwork and in the valuable comments which he made on the draft. Mrs Veronica Chesher has been most helpful in placing her library at my disposal, in discussing Cornish industrial history and in commenting on the earlier report.

All historians of Cornwall are forever in debt to the writings and manuscript collection of Charles Henderson (1900–1933), prince of Cornish scholars, whose many special interests included Cornish woodland.[1]

Oliver Rackham
Corpus Christi College, Cambridge
September 2009

Foreword

Long before I first visited the woods of the Helford River they seemed unusually romantic, no doubt because I still felt the afterglow of Daphne du Maurier's *Frenchman's Creek*. They line the steep valley sides overlooking the river and extend up its tributaries to form a closely linked network of woods dissecting the plateau. Upstream they run as narrow strips surrounding the headwaters, but sea-level rise has drowned the lower river and forced the woods aside, leaving Frenchman's Creek itself as a shrouded inlet on the south side of a yacht-studded natural marina. Today, they provide the backcloth for a broad and winding arm of the English Channel where it is possible to watch jellyfish pulsing away below the overhanging oaks of ancient woodland.

This book was written by Oliver Rackham, a botanist from Cambridge who has transformed our understanding of the history of the British countryside in general and its woodlands in particular. In several remarkably readable volumes, starting with *Trees and Woodland in the British Landscape* and continuing with *Ancient Woodland, The History of the Countryside* and *Woodlands* in the New Naturalist series, he informed and enthused amateurs and professionals alike about our native woodlands, their origins and evolution, how they have been used, and how people have interacted with their natural characteristics to leave us with a scatter of ancient woods, each one both a testimony to its history and an expression of our natural environment.

He first wrote this account of the Helford River woods in 1986, then revised and supplemented it in later years. Oliver clearly intended that it should be published, but it remained incomplete when he died in 2015 and we will never know how much he would have added or changed in final revision. The version he left contained several questions to himself that clearly point to further work on detail, but the substance is consistent with his later writings elsewhere, so, save for some limited subediting, we publish it as he left it.

Books about local groups of woods are rarely published. Publishers, understandably, look for a wide readership, whereas local-interest publications rarely appeal far beyond their locality. Further, modern fashion favours bland and generalised books, so those packed with specialist detail risk outlasting their readership's attention span. Oliver, however, was the exception that proved the rule. He not only published books about single places (*Hayley Wood*; *The Last Forest*, i.e. Hatfield Forest) and localised groups of woods (*The Woods of South-East Essex*), but filled them with detail. They have been widely read because his clear prose, laced with touches of humour and hints of asperity, made the detail not just palatable, but valuable and informative to both specialists and his wider readership. Even his local writings had general significance.

The ancient woods of the Helford River are dominated, almost throughout, by oak, most of which is sessile oak. They form a link in a chain of 'western oakwoods' that runs from Sutherland down the western seaboard to the Helford River and beyond into western Ireland, Brittany and Galicia, being particularly common in Argyll, Cumbria and North Wales. Oakwoods can also be found in all other regions of Britain, including the Boreal zone, where they occur mixed with Highland pinewoods, and the eastern Lowlands, where oak-dominated woodland forms one of the wide range of woodland types in Lincolnshire and East Anglia. The 'eastern' oakwoods, however, are beyond the oceanic climate that gives the western oakwoods their rich assemblages of ferns, bryophytes and lichens, though outliers of such western oakwoods can be found in the Weald and New Forest. With few exceptions, oakwoods occupy strongly acid soils, often peaty. The oaks are accompanied by birches, rowan and, on the less infertile soils, hazel. At their most extreme, they become a form of heathland, with heather, bracken and not much else growing below the oaks. In many places, holly has developed as a dense underwood, notably in the New Forest, Staverton Park, Ebernoe Common and many oakwoods on the western seaboard. Latterly, rhododendron has spread so strongly in some districts that even the holly has been excluded. Oak woodland often grades into ash-elm-hazel woodland on the richer soils and alder-sallow-ash woodland on wet ground, both with broad or narrow transition zones according to topography.

But, how natural are these woods? Oakwoods supported important industries. Charcoal was made on hearths that can still be seen in the woods, and used in metal-working. Bark was stripped from trees that were about to be felled and this was used to tan leather. Ecologists regard them as sort of natural, but I have long thought of them – and the Chiltern beechwoods – as perhaps the least natural of the woodland types we label 'semi-natural'. As with the beechwoods, the dominant species is certainly native, but there is often evidence that the current dominance of oak (or beech) was preceded by a period when oak (or beech) was merely one component of a mixture, and in some cases we know that they were planted as oakwoods (or beechwoods). The oakwoods, in fact, appear to be one of several instances where mixed woodland has been simplified by various means to favour the most useful species.

In the case of some western oakwoods we have historical and pollen evidence that the dominance of oak is a relatively modern phenomenon. They have developed into a landscape that was more wood-pasture-with-oaks than actual closed-canopy, oak-dominated woodland. Some were certainly planted, but oak could easily have regenerated naturally within and around such woodland pasture, and either way there would be little meaningful distinction between ancient and recent woodland. Even if they were dense woodland, the woodmen could have generated oak dominance by careful protection of young oaks or by removing the competition. Thus, for example, in the early 1980s, in one of the Duchy woodlands elsewhere in Cornwall, I once watched a woodman stripping bark for the Grampound tannery and heard from him that the other, less valuable trees and shrubs, such as hazel, were cut out to favour oak.

So, in the case of the Helford River woods, one might expect that, whilst oak is native, the current oak dominance is due as much to people as to natural forces, yet Oliver, who examined historical records, archaeological features and the evidence in the forms of the trees themselves, says little about this. He records no instances of planting oak into ancient woods and makes no mention of selective cutting to favour oaks. He does record ancient coppice stools that demonstrate that particular oak trees have been present for centuries, and mentions remnants of wood-pasture. Further, he describes zonations of woodland types within the ancient woods with the implication that these are natural. Perhaps, then, the Helford River oakwoods are exceptional. It would be worth looking into this further, searching for any evidence that composition has been modified to favour oak. However, it is always possible that some habitual and unspoken aspects of woodmanship would have gone unrecorded if they had no immediate financial consequences and never became the subject of disputes.

There is another aspect of the Helford woodlands that Oliver touches on that might usefully be investigated in greater detail. Many of Britain's present-day native woods originated as plantations or by natural colonisation of open ground after 1600 and thus count as secondary woodland. Some around the area are prominent contributors to the diversity of the Helford River landscape, especially those on the plateau, and their beeches and other trees contribute to the variety of colour, especially in late spring. Others have expanded from the margins of the ancient woods onto sloping or otherwise inconvenient land that ceased to be used as farmland. Both kinds of secondary woodland have ecological interest, partly because they can show how quickly woodland plants and animals spread. Some develop quickly, notably the new woodland that fills the narrow strips of bottom land within the woods, and these add to the diversity of ancient woods. Given enough time, the ancient and the secondary woods may become indistinguishable, as beech, sycamore and others spread into ancient woods and the ancient woodland species colonise new woodland, thereby forming new combinations that will become part of the character and history of the district. Landscapes always change; never repeat.

This is a specialised book about a small group of woods in a remote corner of Britain and, as such, easily regarded as parochial. But much of our understanding of British woods and their context is made up of local studies, such as Steven and Carlisle's *Native Pinewoods of Scotland* (1959), Colin Tubbs' *New Forest* (1968), the Coppins' account of Atlantic hazelwoods (2012) for the Hazel Action Group, Kilmartin, and articles in the *Journal of Ecology* by Donald Pigott (1969) and Francis Merton (1970) on the woodlands of the Derbyshire limestone.* Each adds to our understanding of the wider patterns and processes that have shaped our environment. Here, Oliver Rackham provides us with another detailed, worked example that will help us understand woods elsewhere.

George Peterken
St Briavels Common
March 2018

* Merton, L. F. H. (1970) 'The history and status of the woodlands of the Derbyshire limestone' *Journal of Ecology* 58 pp. 723–744.

Pigott, C. D. (1969) 'The status of *Tilia cordata* and *Tilia platyphyllos* on the Derbyshire limestone' *Journal of Ecology* 57 pp. 491–504.

All other references in George Peterken's Foreword are included in the Bibliography, references and notes (from page 163).

Editorial

After Oliver Rackham's untimely death in February 2015 he left behind a number of manuscripts in various stages of completion. *Ancient Woodland of England: The Woods of the Helford River* was the most complete, although lacking any associated maps, diagrams and photographs. It is almost entirely about the ancient woods of the Helford River area, with occasional reference for comparison to some of the many recent secondary woods in the area.

Oliver's close friend and colleague, Jennifer Moody, gathered together friends and colleagues of Oliver to work on some of these manuscripts, often people who had some connection with, or knowledge of, the works. I had read an earlier draft of *Helford River* which Oliver had lent me in the late 1990s, when he was unofficially supervising my PhD on the historical ecology of woods in Warwickshire. I contacted Jenny Moody to see if she knew what was happening about the *Helford River* and *Woods of South-East Wales* manuscripts. She put me in touch with Paula Keen and Simon Leatherdale, and we set to work to prepare *Helford River* for publication.

We were fortunate to find a photocopy of an early 1987 edition of a report Oliver wrote on the Helford River woods for Kerrier District Council in Cornwall in his archives at Corpus Christi College. This has various diagrams, some of which were suitable to be scanned for the book and others which had to be recreated by me as the photocopy was not entirely of printable quality. Photographs for the book came from Oliver's scanned slides and digital collection in the Corpus archive, as well as from recent visits to the Helford River by Simon Leatherdale, George Peterken and Paul Holley, and from Pamela Tompsett's collection.

George Peterken in his Foreword points out an area of disagreement between him and Oliver. Oliver felt that, from his research into the woods, the pure oakwoods were largely natural; George Peterken feels that weeding by woodmen may account for their present fairly uniform state. I remember discussing with Oliver in the 1990s how significant 'weeding' of trees had been in the past in modifying the composition of semi-natural ancient woods. Oliver was generally very sceptical about it. With woods as long unmanaged as the Helford River woods I think he would have felt that natural processes and colonisation since would probably have radically reduced any effects of such weeding, if indeed it had been employed in the Helford River woods. We leave it to the reader to decide which is the more convincing argument!

A potentially very contentious subject is invasion of the ancient woods by the descendants of planted introduced trees like beech and sycamore, still at an early stage in many woods. Oliver clearly felt they were incompatible with the conservation of the ancient character of the woods as long-coppiced sessile oakwoods; beech is especially aggressive and likely to shade out and destroy old oak coppice. As Oliver says (*see* page 151): 'The beechwood which would be the ultimate result is well represented in other parts of England, is not specially Cornish, and lacks the character and meaning of the ancient oakwoods.' By contrast, George Peterken, in his Foreword, envisages a more benign future for the woods where the invaders form new combinations with the long-established species. Decisions on what to do about complex matters like these will need to be made, on ecological and aesthetic grounds, by the owners and managers of the woods at some point in the not too distant future; simply doing nothing, and hence allowing these man-introduced species to continue increasing, is itself a radical decision with undoubtedly important and possibly very damaging consequences for the woods, as Oliver points out.

The last manuscript version of *Helford River* is dated September 2009 and Oliver's last visit there seems to have been September 2007, so those are the dates to bear in mind when reading the book. As George Peterken says in his Foreword, we have chosen to publish the manuscript very much as Oliver left it with only minor editing. It has been a great privilege to have helped make this work available to the public.

Oliver's work is an important and timely examination of the history, ecology and possible future of the woods of the Helford River and surrounding area, and a valuable addition to his wonderfully readable and informative body of published works.

Acknowledgements

I am very grateful to Paula Keen of the Woodland Trust and Simon Leatherdale, formerly with the Forestry Commission, who have worked with me on the manuscript. Simon also provided photographs for the book and the Index. Also many thanks to Jennifer Moody, copyright owner of the manuscript, who has greatly helped and encouraged along the way; Oliver Padel, who made many thorough and helpful comments on the manuscript and provided digital images of the nineteenth-century OS maps of the Helford River area; Susan Ranson for help proofreading the text; Lucy Hughes, archivist at Corpus Christi College, for access to, and help with, Oliver's archive; and George Peterken for his Foreword and providing photographs.

I should also like to thank: Adrian Cooper at Little Toller books; Timothy Harvey-Samuel, bursar of Corpus Christi College, Cambridge, and one of the executors of Oliver's will; Stuart Laing, Master of Corpus Christi College, Cambridge; Beccy Speight, Michelle Byrne, Helen Dye and Nick Atkinson of the Woodland Trust; the National Trust in Cornwall; Kurt and Caroline Jackson for use of the *Oak and Hazel, Helford* painting for the cover picture; Colin Hawke, former Tree Officer for Cornwall County Council; Pamela Tompsett; Paul Holley for making a special detour to take photographs in the Helford woods while on holiday in Cornwall; and Keith McNaught, who started it all off for me by putting me in touch with Jennifer Moody back in 2015.

David Morfitt
Rugby, Warwickshire
June 2018

Conventions

Any words printed in ***bold italic*** are defined in the Glossary (*see* page 173).

Soil characteristics (e.g. pH) are measured at a depth of 6 inches [15 cm] below the surface of the mineral soil.

Chronological Periods in Britain

Last glaciation (Weichselian): *c.*100,000–12,000 BC
Post-glacial alias present interglacial: *c.*12,000 BC onwards
Palaeolithic: to *c.*10,000 BC
Mesolithic: *c.*10,000–4,500 BC
Neolithic: 4,500–2,200 BC
Bronze Age: 2,200–750 BC
Iron Age: 750 BC–AD 43
Roman: AD 43–410
Dark Ages: AD 410–700
Anglo-Saxon: AD 410–1066
Middle Ages/Medieval: AD 1066–1536 [traditionally 1066–1485]
Post-medieval: AD 1536 onwards [or 1485 onwards]

English Measures and Monetary Equivalents
from Oliver Rackham (1986)a *The History of the Countryside*, Dent, London

1 inch = 25 mm
1 foot = 12 inches = 0.30 m
1 yard = 3 feet = 0.91 m
1 modern perch = 16.5 feet = 5.0 m
1 mile = 1760 yards = 1.6 kilometres
1 modern acre = 4840 square yards = 0.40 hectares
1000 modern acres = 4.0 km2
(The acre is a rectangle measuring 40 x 4 perches. The historic perch could vary from 15.5 feet, as at Little Gransden, Cambridgeshire (Ely Coucher Book), to 30 feet, as at Rufford, Nottinghamshire. Local historic acres could therefore vary from 0.88 to 3.30 modern acres.)
1 cubic foot = 0.028 m3
1 ton = 1.0 t
1 penny (*d*) = £0.0042
1 shilling (*s*) = 12*d* = £0.05

Map References

Map references to Great Britain's National Grid, which is used on all Ordnance Survey (OS) maps, were added by the editor to clarify the locations of woods and obscure historic sites (e.g. sw716260 for Bonallack Wood or sw693287 for Grambla Wood). OS maps for the Helford River area are broadly available in the UK at libraries and booksellers; digital versions are also available online.

Annotated Maps (AM) refer to the 6-inch OS maps that Oliver Rackham used and marked during his fieldwork at the Helford River. The thick line on each of these maps marks the limit of ancient woodland.

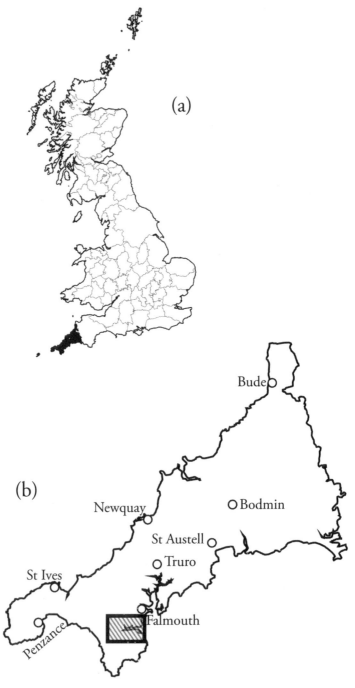

Fig. 1.1 (a) Location of county of Cornwall (in black) and (b) Helford River study area (hatched box), David Morfitt (henceforth DM) 2018.

1 Introduction

There is serious danger that the bulk of the deciduous woods in East Cornwall will be replaced by forests of such trees as western hemlock – trees that have their own beauty as well as great economic value, but which would destroy the characteristic beauty of such places as the Glynn Valley, including the varied carpet of flowers that thrives under deciduous trees ...

The little oaks of Helford Estuary are an essential part of one of the most cherished scenes in the West Country; and they had a sound economic justification in the days when they were used for tin-smelting ...

W. Arnold Foster, *The Listener*, 5 August 1948

THE HELFORD RIVER IN CORNWALL is a place of wonder and delight: one of the very few places in England where **ancient woodland** meets the sea (Fig. 1.1, 1.2). This is oak country, and the oaks have that surprising variety of size and shape that only Cornwall and Devon oaks can offer. Smooth wooded hillsides, subtly mottled with the different greens or browns of individual oak trees, sweep down to high-water mark. The coast is a series of branching drowned valleys, submerged by rising sea level after the end of the last Ice Age. The last trees hang down over the low cliffs or, in the **pills** and little creeks, grow out horizontally for forty feet over the water. To the few people who set foot in the woods are revealed hillsides of bluebells, jungles of holly, sudden headlong ravines and bottomless swamps of golden saxifrage. Polypody fern grows far overhead in the crowns of giant corkscrew oaks ninety feet high. A few yards away, on the other side of a ridge, the oaks are so dwarf that a tall man looks out over their tops. Ribbons of woodland, dark and complicated and often impenetrable, run from the side-creeks up the valleys and far into the hills.

The apparently timeless qualities of this landscape were celebrated by Daphne du Maurier in *Frenchman's Creek*. In spring or winter, in places where the estuary is wooded on both sides, where seaweed catches in the boughs of living trees at high water, and where layers of great oaks

Fig. 1.2 'Where woods meet the sea...'
Merthen Wood West, May 2016 (photograph by S. Leatherdale).

lie on top of each other where they fell into the mud of the pills, one can imagine that just so did the Helford River look when Mesolithic men paddled upon it. This is probably true but much else has happened here, and the present scene is post-industrial as well as aboriginally rustic. Three centuries ago the Helford was a busy place and much less wooded; Frenchman's Creek was bordered with heaths and fields, not with woodland. Such woods as existed were actively growing and being cut down. Ships unloaded at Gweek and Merthen Hole. The whole area reeked with charcoal-hearths and fumed with arsenic from tinworks.

In the twentieth century, residents and visitors feared that this much-loved scene would not last. It narrowly escaped two kinds of physical destruction: in the 1930s from urbanisation à la Bournemouth and in the 1950s from modern forestry. Foster (above) only too accurately predicted the fate of most of the Glynn Valley (Cardinham) and other places in East Cornwall: his only error was to suppose, as foresters did then, that the planted trees would have 'great economic value'. The Second World War, and then the Town and Country Planning Act prevented urbanisation from spreading much beyond Porthnavas Creek. Most of the Helford woods belonged to private owners who saved them from modern forestry. However, there have also been fears that the wooded landscape is self-destroying: that it has not been actively managed for many years; that it is deteriorating and will, in course of time, lose its distinctive character or even disappear altogether; and that human intervention, maybe of a drastic kind, is needed to save it. Are these fears well founded?

How woods work

It is often said that 'the woods of Cornwall were cut down for fuel to smelt tin', as if this explained why the county has not much woodland. This view has been repeated from author to author for over two hundred years:

> Another reason of the scarcity of woods is, that blowing of tin (that is, melting it with wood fire), has much diminished and consumed our wood with charking.
>
> W. Borlase, *The Natural History of Cornwall*, 1758

But this view is a fallacy and not even Borlase's authority makes it right. As we shall see, the Helford River woods have indeed been cut down – many times – for this purpose, but this has not diminished them. Woodland is the natural vegetation of Cornwall and cannot so easily be prevented from growing.

In Cornwall there are ancient woods, natural recent woods and **plantations**. Ancient woods are those that have been in existence since before about 1600. Many are recorded in the **Middle Ages**. One is tempted to suppose that they have never been other than woodland and are direct successors to the **wildwood** of early prehistory, although, as we shall see, there are occasional indications that the story is more complex.

23

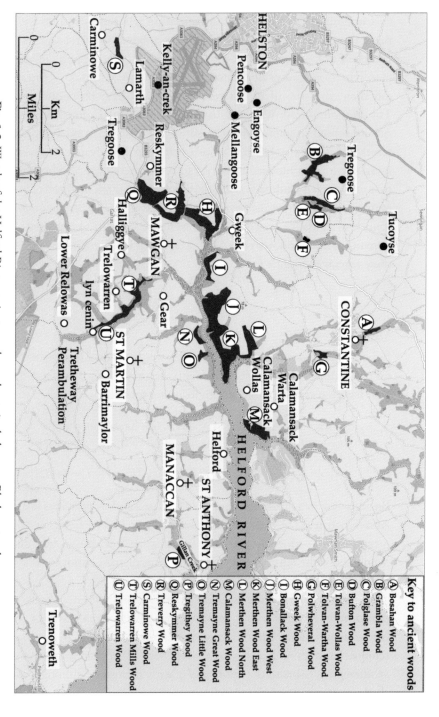

Fig. 1.3 Woods of the Helford River: ancient woods are shown in dark green. Black spots: place-names indicating former woodland. Circles: other places mentioned in the text. Light green: natural recent woods and plantations. (DM 2018 after Rackham 1987; base map © OpenStreetMap contributors.)

Key to ancient woods

Ⓐ Bosahan Wood
Ⓑ Grambla Wood
Ⓒ Polglase Wood
Ⓓ Buffon Wood
Ⓔ Tolvan-Wollas Wood
Ⓕ Tolvan-Wartha Wood
Ⓖ Polwheveral Wood
Ⓗ Gweek Wood
Ⓘ Bonallack Wood
Ⓘ Merthen Wood West
Ⓙ Merthen Wood East
Ⓚ Merthen Wood North
Ⓛ Calamansack Wood
Ⓜ Tremayne Great Wood
Ⓝ Tremayne Little Wood
Ⓞ Tregithey Wood
Ⓟ Reskymner Wood
Ⓠ Treverry Wood
Ⓡ Carminowe Wood
Ⓢ Trelowarren Mills Wood
Ⓣ Trelowarren Wood

24

The main subject of this book is the 25 or so ancient woods, totalling some 600 acres, or 240 hectares, of West Cornwall. Most of these are on the Helford River, but I have included some outliers (Fig. 1.3).

Almost any land, especially in West Cornwall, tends to become woodland unless actively prevented by cultivation, grazing or burning. For example, the fields north of Merthen Wood in summer are full of oak seedlings among the corn, and even one year without ploughing would send them on the way to becoming an oakwood. Two centuries ago, almost every inch of West Cornwall, except the ancient woods, was either cultivated or grazed. Since then there have been times when heathland, fens, roadside verges and the less good farmland have been neglected and allowed to turn into natural *secondary woodland*. Such recent woods have grown bigger in extent than the ancient woodland; they form ribbons along the bottoms of many valleys, sometimes filling an entire valley. In them are the remains of farmsteads, watermills, furnaces, orchards and hundreds of tiny fields.

Plantations are the result of people planting trees, usually trees not indigenous to the area, such as beech (probably not native to Cornwall; *see* page 73), sweet chestnut or various conifers. Plantations may turn into natural woodland by neglect or by the planted trees not surviving and wild trees taking their place. Conversely, natural woods (ancient or recent) may be made into plantations by replanting – destroying the indigenous trees and replacing them by planted trees.

Our ancient woods, like most in England, are *coppices*. Oak and most other native trees, when cut down, do not die but sprout from the stump, which becomes a permanent base called a stool and can be cut again and again to yield successive crops of poles (Fig. 1.4). After centuries of cutting and regrowth the stool becomes a giant stool which may be 10 ft [3.05 m] or more across. Some species – we are concerned with cherry, service, and some elms – instead of coppicing produce suckers from the roots; they grow in ever-widening circular patches called clones.

Under traditional woodmanship an ancient wood was self-renewing and produced two distinct products: timber and *underwood*. Every year, or every few years, part of the wood was cut down to yield underwood, coppice poles or sucker poles which were the main and regular product. Underwood had many uses, but we are chiefly concerned with it as fuel. In this area of Cornwall it grows slowly and was cut at rather

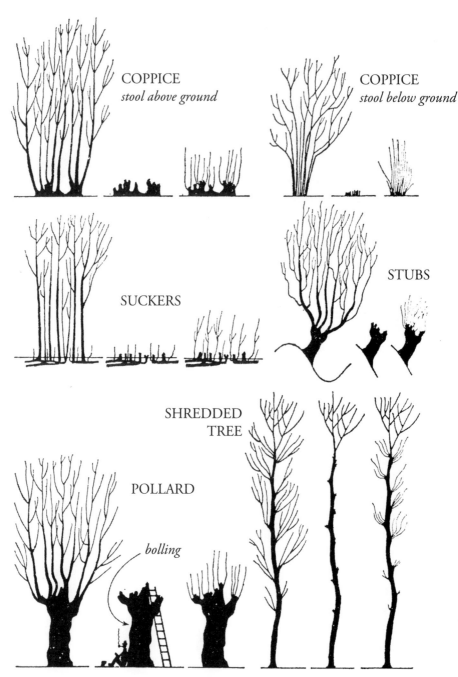

COPPICE
stool above ground

COPPICE
stool below ground

SUCKERS

STUBS

SHREDDED
TREE

POLLARD

bolling

Fig. 1.4 Ways of managing wood-producing trees. For each method, the tree, or group of trees, is shown just before cutting, just after cutting, and one year after cutting. All drawn to the same scale. (Originally published in Rackham 1976; reproduced courtesy of Jennifer Moody.)

long intervals of perhaps thirty years. Most woods also had **timber** or **standard** trees, usually oaks, allowed to grow through several cycles of the underwood and then felled to provide beams and planks. Coppicing in origin goes back to the Neolithic period; in Cornwall it was already established by the time of the earliest medieval records.

Even in neglect, an ancient wood preserves the characteristic multi-stemmed structure of coppicing. Plantations and recent woods usually have only one stem per tree.

Coppice-woods are not quite the whole story. In a few places there are remains of **wood-pasture**, where the trees are widely spaced, allowing grass or heather to grow between them. Historical references to cattle or sheep feeding in 'woods' must mean wood-pasture. Wood-pasture trees were often treated as **pollards**, cut high enough above the ground for the animals not to be able to browse the regrowth. Such trees tend to become long-lived 'veteran' trees, of special **conservation** value because of the peculiar animals (bats, special insects) and rare lichens that live on them.

Significance of the West Cornwall woods

These woods are the south-west tip of the great belt of Atlantic oakwoods that runs through Devon and Wales and northern England into south-west Scotland and ending in Argyll, but with outliers as far north as Inverness and also scattered over Ireland. Distinctively, most of the trees are oaks, timber and underwood alike; and the oaks tend to be of the 'sessile' species, *Quercus petraea*. These woods contrast with the greater variety of tree species characteristic of lowland England, where oaks tend to be more thinly scattered as timber trees only, and are nearly always of the 'pedunculate' species, *Quercus robur*. This is a fundamental distinction and was established in the time of the prehistoric wildwood.

Wood-pasture is part of a worldwide tradition, which is widespread in the tropics under the name of **savanna**. It barely extends into Cornwall, although there is one famous example in the ancient deer-park of Boconnoc.

2 Environment: geology and soils

The Helford is not a proper river but a valley drowned by the sea. The woods are on its steep sides, sloping sometimes at more than 45 degrees. Most of the woods extend a little way on to the plateau at the top; some have internal valleys (Fig. 6.4).

The land usually ends in a wave-cut cliff up to 30 ft [9.14 m] high. Although the land is now sinking at about an inch [2.5 cm] every twelve years,[2] the cliffs do not appear to be actively eroding. Possibly the cliffs remain from a higher sea-level in the past; this is confirmed by there being a double cliff below Bonallack Wood.

Geology

The bedrock under the Helford River itself and most of the woods is Gramscatho Beds, of Devonian age, appearing mainly as much-shattered slates. Some of the outlying woods lie either southwards in the Meneage Crush Zone, of great geological complexity, or northwards on the edge of the Carnmenellis granite (Fig. 2.1).

The soils were formed partly by the weathering of rocks on the spot, and partly from material slithering down the slopes when it was freezing and thawing late in the last Ice Age. Another component is loess, dust blown from a distance by the wind, also at the end of the last Ice Age. Loess forms much of the soils on the Lizard plateau;[3] around the Helford River it is less clearly visible, but I have seen an example on the plateau near Helford and it probably forms the silt content of woodland soils.

Soils

The northern Helford woods

The soils in these woods are of the brown-earth class. They are at least moderately acid, often well drained (for woodland soils), and more or less infertile.

The woods from Gweek to Calamansack show three zones. The edge of the plateau has deep, brown, silty clay soils which are usually very acid and moderately infertile. The upper slopes, often brackeny with patches of holly and hazel, have orange silty-clayey, often stony, shallow, rather less acid soils. On the bottom slopes there is a heathy zone, with evidently very infertile soils on a yellow or orange poorly drained acid clay. In Calamansack Wood the top zone (Fig. 6.2) has pH readings of 3.8–3.9, with one value of 5.7 where the vegetation indicates a small patch of greater fertility; the middle zone has pH 4.1– 4.7; the lower zone 4.0. Tremayne Great Wood tells a less consistent story, with pH of 4.0 at the top of the wood and 3.7 halfway down.*

The three zones are consistent in wood after wood, and evidently result from natural processes operating down the slope on a relatively uniform bedrock. Loess and other materials have crept, slithered or been washed downslope; minerals have been leached by rainwater or have migrated downhill in dead leaves. In most sloping woods the bottom becomes more fertile than the top; this has not happened here, probably because the downslope movement continues into the sea.

Humus is nearly all of the leaf mould type, in which dead leaves pile up on the surface from year to year and rot down gradually to form a separate layer of organic mould called mor. The soils are too acid for the earthworms, which in 'ordinary' soils drag dead leaves into their burrows and prevent them from accumulating as leaf mould. Earthworm soils, in which the humus (called mull) is mixed into the top layer of mineral soil, occur here only in pockets of less acidity. On the lower slopes, humus and minerals tend to be washed out of the upper mineral soil and deposited in a lower layer.[4] This process, podzolisation, depends partly on the vegetation; it happens more easily under heathland than woodland. Soils here are probably not acid enough for a podzol to have been induced by the oakwoods themselves. More likely it was made by heather and bilberry, plants which release podzolising chemicals and which would have flourished after each coppicing. I have not found podzols under holly, which has the reputation of being a de-podzolising tree.

---

* pH is a measure of acidity. In soils it ranges from 3.0, the most acid, to 8.0, the most alkaline. Most woodland soils have pH between 3.5 and 7.0.

Fig. 2.1 Geology of the Helford River area. From the Quarter-inch geological map of England and Wales, New Series, Sheet number 21 and 25, Sheet title: Bodmin, Truro, Falmouth, Land's End, Isles of Scilly. Reprinted 1969. (British Geological Survey materials © NERC 1969).

In valleys, especially in Merthen Wood, there are waterlogged, peaty soils, sometimes fed by springs from the sides. These appear from the vegetation to be less acid and more fertile.

The southern woods

Soils in the Meneage woods are more variable and sometimes more fertile than those to the north, and do not podzolise. Tremayne Great Wood generally resembles the top zone of Calamansack, with similar vegetation and pH 3.6–4.0; there is less evidence of variation down the slope, and no heathy zone at the bottom. Part of the same slope, however, is elmwood with abundant nettles, indicating an abrupt change to a soil rich in phosphate though still acid (pH 3.8–4.4); springs emerging here suggest a change in the bedrock. Tremayne Little Wood appears to be full of loess.

In Trelowarren Wood the upper slope again has shallow acid soils. On the lower slope, in contrast, these are replaced by moderately fertile, calcareous soils with mull humus (pH 5.1). The slope runs down to a peaty valley. Much the same sequence occurs in Trelowarren Mills Wood, with pH 5.1–5.5 on the mull soils of the lower slope, 5.6–5.8 in the peaty valley floor, and 7.0 in the mud of the main stream (which flows from ultrabasic rocks).

Conclusions

The Trelowarren woods are an example of the 'Highland Zone Catena', to be found in many woods on slopes in Scotland, Wales, Ireland, north and west England. The bedrock is rather infertile; calcium and other minerals are washed out of the upper slopes and edge of the plateau and travel down to enrich the lower slopes. This results in a characteristic sequence of soil and vegetation zones. The northern Helford woods exhibit only the top of the sequence, for the slope runs into the sea. The bedrock is evidently not quite uniform; changes in it probably account for patches of greater fertility in Tremayne and Calamansack woods, as well as for the generally lower acidity of the southern woods.

The Soil Survey has produced an elaborate classification of the soils of the Lizard Peninsula, up to the south shore of the Helford River.[5] The southern woods are mapped mainly as the Dartington Series of soils, usually in its deep-soil, steep-slope variant. Dartington Soils are podzolic, stony clay loams over slate; they are widespread in Cornwall and Devon. The valley bottoms are described as 'miscellaneous alluvial' and not discussed further.

Dartington Series is probably the correct classification for the soils of heaths (and former heaths) close to the ancient woods. For the woods themselves on the south side it is inappropriate, as their soils do not have a podzolic tendency. A better category would be the steep-slope variant of the Highweek Series – the usual, non-podzolic, clay loam of the Meneage plateau.

On the north side, the upper parts of the woods probably belong also to the Highweek Series or to its poorly-drained equivalent, the Sannan Series. Dartington is represented in the heathy, shallow soils of the lower slopes. In places (especially in Calamansack Wood) these run into deeper, clayey podzols, which are a special type not recorded in the Lizard.

3 History

Wildwood

DURING THE LAST ICE AGE, the British Isles would have been something like the present arctic tundra, in which tree growth was virtually impossible, even in Cornwall. Whether trees were completely absent is a matter for debate. As the climate became warmer, trees returned in a particular sequence, giving rise to a more or less stable wildwood about 7000 years ago. Generally trees seem to have migrated from continental Europe, appearing first in south-east England which was then joined to France. Among the anomalies is that oak seems to have appeared first in Cornwall and migrated north-east, which suggests that a few trees may have survived the glaciation somewhere near Cornwall, perhaps on the extensive area that the then lower sea-level would have exposed between Cornwall, Wales and Scilly.

Wildwood is known chiefly from identifying and counting the tree pollen grains buried in lake muds and peat-bogs. In Cornwall the commonest trees were probably oak, elm and hazel. There would have been tracts of hazelwood on soils of average fertility (Fig. 3.1), with elmwood on the more fertile and oakwood on the less fertile soils. Cornwall thus formed part of the Oak–Hazel Province of west Britain, extending as far as the south-west Scottish Highlands.[6]

There are no long-continued pollen records for West Cornwall, but such evidence as there is for the Lizard points to the great importance of hazel in prehistory.[7] Lime (the native 'small-leaved' lime, *Tilia cordata*), then the commonest tree of south, east and midland England, occurred on the Lizard, though was probably uncommon.

When I first drafted this book in 1986 it was assumed that wildwood was forest: the proverbial squirrel could have leapt from tree-top to tree-top from Land's End at least as far as Inverness. I am not so sure now: in 1998, I pointed out that wildwood pollen deposits contained

Fig. 3.1 Hazelwood in Roskymmer Wood, March 1987.

pollen of plants like devil's-bit that did not flower in shade.[8] In 2000, Francis Vera reconstructed wildwood as a shifting mosaic of patches of woodland set in grassland, maintained by the browsing of deer and wild oxen: the squirrel might have been able to leap at most from Gweek to Calamansack.[9] Although at the time of writing scientific opinion seemed to be shifting against Vera,[10] his reconstruction is unlikely to go away entirely. It explains too much: it explains how deer and wild oxen could have found somewhere to feed; it explains how Neolithic farmers could have transferred themselves, their crops and domestic animals to Britain without having to starve while they were digging up trees to create fields.

The historic state of Cornwall, as a land of oakwoods, results from prehistoric agriculture. Long before the earliest written records, all the elmwoods and nearly all the hazelwoods had been destroyed for farmland. Oakwoods, being on steep slopes and infertile soils, were left till last. Other woodland types survive only on patches of fertile soils within oakwoods. The many elm-groves on the Lizard and elsewhere result from the suckering of farmland elms in recent centuries.[11]

Beech is almost certainly an exotic tree in Cornwall. It may have been here in prehistory, as suggested by fossil pollen, but died out before written records. All the present beeches appear to have been planted in the eighteenth and nineteenth centuries or to be the children of planted trees.

Prehistoric cultures

Neolithic and Bronze Age people made some impact on the Cornish wildwood; we cannot tell how much, because the evidence has been destroyed or confused by millennia of later cultivation. Most of the Bronze Age evidence in the area is well to the south of the Helford River, where the Lizard moors and their surroundings are full of barrows, standing-stones and field systems. North of the Helford such monuments less often survive, though they include spectacular megaliths like The Tolvan (Cornish for 'hole-stone'; Fig. 3.2).

The discovery of two round barrows within what is now ancient woodland indicates that the woods, to some degree, were less extensive in the Bronze Age than in the Middle Ages or today. Barrows, as important tombs, were meant to be seen from a distance and were not hidden in woods. The barrow now within the highest part of Merthen Wood was carefully sited to be seen from across the Helford River; that in Gweek Wood would have attracted the attention of anyone paddling up to the last fork in the river.

There can be no doubt of the Iron Age landscape. Around the Helford River is one of the greatest concentrations in Great Britain of rounds, hillforts and similar structures.[12] Rounds and hillforts are supposed to be Iron Age; the square earthworks (e.g. Merthen Camp) are conjectured to be of Roman date, although continuing the Iron Age tradition. The one such earthwork in our area that has recently been excavated is the square 'round' at Grambla Wood, which produced evidence of Roman and immediately post-Roman occupation.[13]

Whatever the reason for this concentration of warlike earthworks, they imply a large population, and their siting demanded views of the sea. By the Iron Age at the latest, most of the plateau would have been farmland or moorland. Woodland, at most, was by then confined to valleys and seaward slopes. At least seven of the ancient woods of today are immediately beneath rounds or 'camps'.

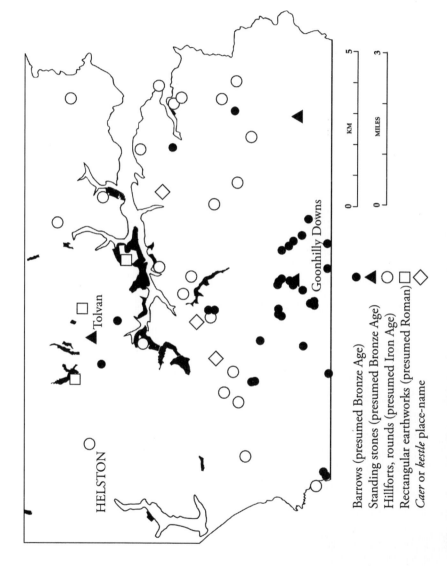

Fig. 3.2 Antiquities of the Helford River in relation to the ancient woods. (DM 2018 after Rackham 1987.)

HELSTON

Tolvan

Goonhilly Downs

● Barrows (presumed Bronze Age)
▲ Standing stones (presumed Bronze Age)
○ Hillforts, rounds (presumed Iron Age)
□ Rectangular earthworks (presumed Roman)
◇ *Caer* or *kestle* place-name

Anglo-Saxon charters

The earliest written descriptions of the countryside are *perambulations*, defining the boundaries of estates when they changed hands. For Cornwall there survive seventeen perambulations in ten charters, dated between AD *c.*939 and 1049, in which the boundary clauses are written in Old English with Cornish place-names. These prove that Cornwall was then not a very wooded land. Woodland is rarely mentioned and many of the lines of sight involved in following the bounds would be possible only in moorland or farmland.[14, 15] For the Lizard there are six perambulations, which show that (then as now) the interior of the peninsula was open moorland, but the northern third was a complex landscape of roads and dykes, densely sprinkled with hamlets and farmsteads. Several of the present farmsteads are indeed named in the charters.[16]

Only in one place does a charter-boundary touch the Helford River woods. The bounds of *Trefdewig* (now Trethewey),[17] dated 977, preserved in the archives of Exeter Cathedral, read thus:

> First at *pennhal meglar*;[a] a south to the way;[b] then on to the ford;[c] straight to *erliwet*;[d] then forth along the stream to *lyncenin*; then up to *pennhal meglar*.

>> a. The place-name means 'end of the moor of *Meglar*', and it is connected with the present-day farm of Barrimaylor (SW737234).
>> b. the road from Newtown (SW741231) in St Martin to Polawyn (SW720228)
>> c. the stream below Trewince (SW735224)
>> d. probably the present farm Lower Relowas (SW728226)

The point *lyn cenin* means 'Pool of the Wild-Garlic', and is evidently in the valley below St Martin church, at what was the inland tip of Trelowarren Wood until its recent extension. Just over a thousand years later, Dr D. E. Coombe found the spot; wild garlic still grows there. The plant is surprisingly uncommon in west Cornish woods (Fig. 3.3).[18]

Domesday Book

William the Conqueror's great survey of 1086 records Cornwall fully: this is the only Celtic land, other than Flintshire, which the survey covers. It records woodland in several ways. For Cornwall it gives measurements of woods, from which the areas can be estimated. These

Fig. 3.3 Wild garlic in Frenchman's Creek, April 2016
(photograph by G. F. Peterken).

add up to 28,000 acres, 3.2 per cent of the county. Cornwall was the least wooded English county outside the Fens. Most of the woods were in the south-east; the west half of Cornwall had barely 1.5 per cent of woodland.

For Kerrier the woodland records are unsatisfactory, because the north side of the Helford River and much of the south side were subsumed in the king's giant manors of Helston and Winnington. Helston, apparently including much of Constantine, is credited with 1 league x ½ league of woodland. The Domesday league was 1.5 miles, so that this area works out at roughly 500 acres. Following the Domesday Book's usual custom, the areas of what may well have been two or more woods on one estate have been combined into one measurement.

The king's estates to the south of the Helford River are assigned to the

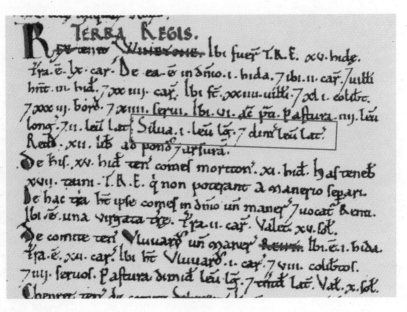

Fig. 3.4 Domesday Book: Winnington, showing woodland 1 x ½ league entry (Credit: Professor John Palmer and George Slater).

manor of Winnington, now a minor farm in Gunwalloe (sw659207), which also had 1 league x ½ league of woodland (Fig. 3.4). The more detailed Exeter version of the text specifies that Winnington's 1 x ½ league was in the sub-manor of Mawgan, and that there were further areas of 6 acres of woodland in Trelowarren and 6 acres in Crawle, as well as 'little groves' (*nemuscula*) of 6 acres in Halliggye (near Trelowarren) and 5 acres in Truthall (in Sithney). Private owners had 12 acres of woodland at Gear and 2 acres at *Tucowit* (Tucoyse in Constantine).

All these woods cannot have added up to much more than 1000 modern acres (even though the acre used by Domesday was probably bigger than that of today). The records of other land-uses in the Helford River area and the Lizard include some 20,000 modern acres of arable and more than 30,000 acres of pasture.[19]

Identifications are uncertain because of the multitude of Cornish place-names and Domesday Book's erratic habits in spelling them. However, it is clear that there was little woodland in West Cornwall in 1086 (none at all in the Penwith peninsula) and in some places remarkably small woods

Domesday place	Location	Domesday woodland	Modern acres	Present State
TREDINTONE	Tehidy in Illogan	1 x 1 league	1000	present Portreath Wood?
BENNARTONE	Binnerton in Crowan	1 x ½ league	500	later divided with 2 other manors, now vanished
MATELE	Methleigh by Porthleven	underwood 60 acres	70	nothing there now
CVDAWOID	Cosawes near Penryn	60 acres	70	present Cosawes Wood
TREWEL	Treliever in Mabe	60 acres	70	present Devichoys Wood?
RITWORE	Roseworthy in Gwinear, west of Camborne	½ league x 2 furlongs	60	nothing there now
TRESCAV	Trescow in Breage	3 acres	3½	
TALGOLLE	Tolgullow near St Day	2 acres	2½	
WORESLYN	Gurlyn in St Erth	underwood 2 acres	2½	westernmost wood in Domesday

Table 1 Other Domesday woods in West Cornwall.

were recorded. Rarely does Domesday Book mention coppice-woods (*silva minuta*) as it does systematically for Lincolnshire and Nottinghamshire.

All of the bigger ancient woods today can be plausibly accounted for in 1086. There were some big woods that have vanished or are now much smaller : thus the great wood of Tehidy in Illogan is reduced to the present wood of Portreath (unless there are remains of other woods among the plantations that surround the former hospital).

Cornwall, along with Devon, is one of the two counties where woodland appears to have increased since Domesday Book. The 3.2 per cent of woodland in 1086 became 3.6 per cent by 1895. The Ancient Woodland Inventory credits Cornwall with 1.9 per cent of ancient woodland in 1930 and, although much of this has been coniferised since, it represents a remarkably high survival rate. In few if any other counties has more than half of the eleventh-century woodland survived into the twentieth century. The survival rate around the Helford River is higher still.

Domesday Book and the charters portray a landscape not very different from the farmed countryside of today, but with rather more woodland than there is now. Woods persisted mainly on steep slopes and other uncultivable spots. Where the records tell us anything about the locations of woods, these are compatible with what is there now (e.g. Trelowarren, Halliggye). At Tucoyse ('Woodside') an accident of ownership – it was the only documented hamlet on the north side of the Helford not belonging to the Crown – has preserved a record of one of the little valley-woods: the '2 acres' of woodland mentioned by Domesday probably still exist as Bufton and Tolvan-Wollas Wood (both of which places later belonged to Tucoyse manor[20]). Similarly the '5 acres' of woodland separately recorded for Truthall may be the present Truthall Wood, close to another place called Tregoose. Even tiny woods are important in Cornish history; records were kept of them and places were named after them.

There are indications from place-names of rather more woodland at some unknown date before 1086. Names such as Tregoose (Cornish *tre* 'hamlet' + *coose* 'wood'), Burncoose, Pencoys or Pencoose ('Woodsend'), Pengelly ('Grovesend'), Mellangoose ('Wood Mill'), and Coswinsawsin (Saxons' White Wood)[21] are occasionally to be found either where there is now no woodland, or where the wood still exists but does not extend so far up the valley. Usually, these are in places where Domesday Book, too, lacks woodland. They are conspicuously absent from Penwith. I infer that although West Cornwall lost most of its woodland in prehistory, there was still some continuing loss in the latter centuries before Domesday.

The Middle Ages

In the next two centuries the great royal estates were broken up. Individual farms and woods emerge from anonymity and appear in records of the Carminowes, Reskymmers, Vyvyans and other Lizard gentry. The physical changes were probably not very great; but, as in the rest of England, we must suppose that the population increased and with it the demand for land. Slopes previously thought uncultivable were grubbed out and farmed. The climax of this expansion, and for a long time the minimum woodland area, would have been reached by the date of the Black Death in 1349.

Woods were valuable private property. This is shown by a thirteenth-century agreement subdividing rights in a wood called Kelliancrek between the lords of Carminowe and Reskymmer.[22] Part of the wood belonged to the Carminowe farm of Lamarth and part to the Reskymmer farm of Tregoose. Probably it lay somewhere up the valley from the surviving Carminowe Wood (Fig. 1.3). *Kelly-an-crek* is a Cornish wood-name meaning Barrow Grove; after the wood disappeared the place-name survived (as 'Kelly Anchor Farm') until Culdrose airfield swallowed it.[23, 24]

The records refer clearly to the three ancient woods still surviving on the north side of the Helford River, beginning with Calamansack. In 1249, Bartholomew and Isabella de Chamond successfully pursued a claim against Richard Williamson:

> to have in the woods of the said Richard at Kylmoncote ... reasonable estovers for the repairs of their houses & their mills at their manor of Trenowyd, and to fill up their hedges & also reasonable estovers for firewood at the said manor of Trenowyd.[25]

The tenurial history shows that *Kylmoncote* is Calamansack – the name is probably not that of the wood itself but of the nearby hamlet (*see* pages 7 and 107). *Trenowyd* is Trenoweth in St Keverne, far away across the Helford River. Estovers are customary rights to the produce of someone else's wood; here they imply both timber (houses and mills) and underwood (hedges and firewood).

Bonallack Wood is named from the barton of Bonallack, mentioned in 1386 as *Benadlek*; the name means 'Broomy (place)' and is probably that of the farm, although broom does grow in the wood itself. The wood is mentioned in the 1390s as the wood of *Banathelek*.[26]

In the 1390s, Merthen Manor, with its wood, was divided between two heirs:

> John Aroundell shall have the third part of the wood of *Merthyn* next the wood of *Benathelek*, except 6 acres next *Merthyn*, together with all the wood of *Trelewytha*[a] ... John Trevarthian shall have the said manor of *Merthyn*, and the two parts and 6 acres of the wood of the same manor ... The said John Aroundell shall enclose his [share] of the wood of *Merthyn* ... [27]
>
> a. Far away in St Mewan.

At this time Merthen Wood was continuous with Bonallack Wood. The Aroundell share probably lay to the west of the ravine which now lies just inside the west end of the wood (*see* page 158, Fig. AM1). This was evidently thought to be one-third less six acres of the whole wood, although it would really have been rather less. Most of it was grubbed out some two hundred years later, but the tithe survey of Constantine parish in 1842 names the remaining part 'Arundell Wood'; it then belonged to the inland hamlet of Nancenoy. The name was still used in the twentieth century.[28] The part that remains, with its great savanna-like oaks, is one of the two survivors of wood-pasture in West Cornwall.

In Cornwall even small woods had names of their own in the Cornish language – unlike Wales and other Celtic countries, where most woods merely took the name of the farm that owned them. Not many of these names survive in use; Devichoys and Cosawes woods are examples.

Merthen Wood was regarded as three separate woods, each with a *coose* name. A deed of 1389 mentions 'Coesenys, a wood adjoining the Wood of Benathelek' – evidently what was to become Arundell Wood. Charles Henderson found the name Coose-Carmynowe and Cosabnack given to parts of Merthen Wood. These seem to be Merthen East and West and Arundell Woods. The names mean 'Island Wood', 'Carminowe Wood', and 'Something-y Wood': the medieval Cornish (like the English, e.g. Isle of Purbeck) could see islands in the landscape where you and I cannot. As we shall see, part of Merthen Wood was still under Carminowe jurisdiction in the sixteenth century; another part belonged to Winnington in Gunwalloe, more than five miles away.

Among valley woods away from the Helford River we have already noted *Kelly-an-crek*. Henderson quotes thirteenth-century references to Penrose Wood (the present Oak Wood by the Loe Pool) and Penventon Wood (somewhere nearby).[29]

Woodmanship

The conservative tradition of managing woods began in the Neolithic[30] and by the Middle Ages was established throughout England. Whenever a tree was cut down it was expected to be replaced, either by growth from the stump or roots or by a new seedling.

A county like Cornwall, which had inherited very little woodland, might be expected to attach special importance to conservation. The owners of Clowance in c.1210 and c.1233 endowed the Priory of St Michael's Mount with supplies from their grove at Clowance. The earlier grant includes a weekly cartload of wood, implying regular coppicing; the later mentions large and small timber for maintaining buildings, besides underwood in the form of hazel rods and rods for thatching.[31]

The earliest reference to Calamansack Wood in 1249 implies that the wood was producing underwood and timber on a permanent basis. It was supplying a distant place in the Lizard Peninsula, which had little or no woodland of its own.

In 1489, the court of Winnington Manor visited Merthen Wood to investigate a charge that:

> Richard Tom Ude cut down oaks in the Lord's wood of Mirthyn on Monday [27 April 1489] to the value of 4s. without permission ...[32]

There was a similar case in the Carminowe part of the wood in 1570.[33] Down the centuries, the records imply that the chief product of the woods was fuel. Timber is not often mentioned, though we can hardly doubt that the woods did produce a little; it would not have grown well except in valleys (see pages 79–80). There are one or two medieval references to *pannage*, the fattening of pigs in years when there was an acorn crop, which was one of the rights in *Kelly-an-crek*; as in most of England, this was only a minor and undependable woodland product.

The fate of the woods

By 1500 the woods on the Helford River amounted to little more than the 400-odd acres of ancient woodland that still exist. There were at most 150 acres of woods, like Bufton, hidden in inland valleys. In the wider area there were Cosawes and Devichoys Woods,[34] with their Cornish wood-names, and others around Penryn now vanished, such as Restronguet Wood – perhaps another 300 acres. In Crowan there had earlier been the adjacent woods of Clowance, Binnerton, and Drym;[35] some 50 acres of these may perhaps still have existed in 1500.[36] All these could have added up to no more than 1000 acres of woodland in the whole of Kerrier and Penwith, about 0.5 per cent of the land area. This would not have been enough for the ordinary domestic requirements of fuel, wood and timber, let alone for the demands of industry. Most of West Cornwall must have burnt peat, or furze, or coal from South Wales.

Many ancient buildings in Cornwall have timbers of elm,[37] which is unlikely to have come from woodland trees.

Sixteenth and seventeenth centuries

One of the earliest large-scale maps in England depicts the approaches to Falmouth Harbour in *c.*1545. It roughly but unmistakeably shows Calamansack, Merthen and Gweek Woods, as well as Restronguet Wood (now vanished) and other woods around Penryn.[38]

Merthen Wood

John Leland, visiting Cornwall at about this time, describes Merthen.

> Morden, where Mr Reskimer hath a ruinus maner place, and a fair park well woddid; wherof 3 partes[a] is within the principal streme of the haven, and a creke caullid Poole Penvith, hemmid yn … a creke of salt water, caullid Poulpere, and hemmith in a peace of Mr Reskymer's Parke at Merdon, so that with this creke, and the main se water of the haven, upon a 3 partes[a] the parke is strenkthyd.[b] Poul Wheverel about half a mile lower, having a brooke resorting to it. There is on the same side halfe a mile [lower] another creke callid Cheilow, alias Chalmansak.[39]

> a. sides
> b. strengthened (referring to the park perimeter)

We recognise Polwheveral Creek and its branch to Polpenwith; Calamansack Creek is now called Porthnavas. Poulpere [Clean Pool] is evidently the name, otherwise unrecorded, of the middle pill of Merthen Wood.[40] Leland's description implies that the deer-park reached the sea and included Merthen Wood, but he may have been misinformed: later surveys clearly state that it did not include the wood.[41 42 43]

In *c.*1580 there was a detailed survey of Merthen. The estate comprised 520¾ acres, including among other lands:

'a fayre gentlemans house wth all office therevnto belonging not* to be erected for [£]60'
'The meadow adioyning wth the west wood'
'The Lawne', 20¾ acres
'The moore betweene the park and the west wood'
'The deare parke itselfe', 79.12 acres, worth £13 3s. 7d. per annum
'The herbadge & pasture of 143 acres and 21 yards [143.13 acres] of Wood land', worth £7 3s. per annum
'The present woods now growing to be sould' worth £100 16s.
'The soyle of the woods after the sheare worth per aker' £190 13s. 4d.[44]

[*scribal error for now?]

The survey seems to be accurate, and the area of the woods agrees remarkably well with the modern acreage of Merthen East and West (but not North) Woods, 143.6 acres. The last three items value (as was then customary) the trees in the woods separately from the soil, and add a small value for the pasturage of the woods. The deer-park evidently comprised the present fields within Merthen Wood, around the ancient earthworks, but not the wood itself (*see* page 160, Fig. AM3). The Lawne lay to the west of the earthworks; the name implies that it had once been part of the park.[45] Other assets included 'a lyme kylne', doubtless the predecessor of the great kiln still to be seen at Merthen Hole; port dues ('Ancoradge keeladge bushelladge & land leave'); and £2 per annum worth of 'Oare [seaweed] to burne for kelpe making'.

Calamansack Wood was put on record because of its history of subdivision. The manor had been divided into Calamansack Wartha and Calamansack Wollas; Wartha (Higher Calamansack) had all the wood, and Wollas (Lower) had all the heath. A deed of 1573 mentions the further division of 'Kyllymansack alias ... Kilmonsack wartha' into two-thirds and one-third.[46] The division got more complicated, and an early-seventeenth-century letter implies at least three owners:

> Worshippfull, we haue heartofore advertysed yor wrshipp, that we had bought mr Rosewarnes pt of his woode in Kyllymonsack ... wch wood is in common wth yours wch is but a smale parte ... if it please you to sell yor pte we will paye you so much as we paied mr Rosewarne.[47]

Then, in the mid-seventeenth century, the wood was surveyed thus:

Callamountsack woode cont 13 Acres euery Acre worth to be sold 40s.
The pasture of euery acre therof worth per an[num] 3s. 4d.
The rem[ain]dr of 6 Acres of this woode are sould by Sr ffrauncis Vivian
at this time eu[ery] Acre for 20s.
… the barke of those 6 Acres Allreddy sold wherof mr Monck is to
haue the 3d parte being [£]2 0s. 0d.[48]

The 19 acres may include only part of the present wood but, as we
shall see, it is possible that the acres are bigger than those now used and
that the whole wood is meant.

The Constantine Survey

An inland wood is mentioned in a woodcutting lease, dated 1604,
and is referred to as 'the enclosed wood at Tucoys'.[49] Later, in 1649,
all the lands in Constantine parish were listed and valued for assessing
the rates.[50] For the Merthen estate the entry includes 'The East and
West Woods' (106 acres), 'Deer Park 5 Plotts' (14 acres), and 'The
Lawn'. 'Arundall Wood' is given as a separate estate of 21 acres but was
apparently no longer a wood. Calamansack Wartha was divided into
two estates, one-twelfth and eleven-twelfths, and its wood (21 acres)
accordingly appears as two entries of 1¾ and 19¼ acres.

In Table 2 I have listed all the woods in the 1649 survey, and have
compared them with those in the Constantine tithe survey of 1842.
The 1649 survey was evidently less rigorous than that of c.1580. It used
a bigger acre. The English acre is a rectangle of 40 perches by 4 but
the perch did not always have its modern value of 16½ feet; perches
of 18 or 21 ft are often encountered and the acres are correspondingly
bigger.[51] All the lands in Constantine in the 1649 survey add up to 4678
acres. On the basis of a 21-ft perch this would be equivalent to 4678
x $(21/16.5)^2$ = 7578 modern acres, a good approximation to the actual
area of the parish (7900 acres in 1841). Merthen farm is given as 307¼
acres, which would be 498 modern acres, comparable with the 520¼
acres given in c.1580. The 1649 survey thus appears to have used a 21-ft
perch and I have scaled the woodland areas accordingly.

Constantine in 1649 had 300 modern acres of woodland, nearly four
per cent of the parish – less than there is now. Four-fifths of it was in
the three big woods of Merthen, Calamansack and Bonallack, then at

Constantine Survey NAME and description	Previous records (if any)	1649 area, acres	1649 area, modern acres[a]	1841 area, acres[b]	Present state
MERTHEN The East and West woods	*boscus de Merthyn* 1386	106	172.0	160.50[c] incl. North Wood	unaltered
BENALLACK The Woods	*boscus de Banathelek* 1390s	18	29.0	19.30[c]	unaltered
TREVIADES A Grove under Park Bush		½	0.8	1.68	still there
TOLVAN-WARTHA The Woods		4	6.5	3 woods, total 11.90	one still there (2.50 acres)
POLWARTHA The Woods		1	1.6		
POLWHEVERELL War[tha] The Woods		8	13.0	13.67	Polwheveral wood
POLWHEVERELL The Woods		1½	2.4	1.12	gone
PENBOTHIDNOW The Wood		1¼	2.0		gone?
TRENGILLY Crofts and Wood		4	6.5		gone?
TUCOOSE Wood [2 Parcels]	*Tvcowit* wood 1086	10	16.0		gone
TOLVAN WOLLAS The Wood	[part of above]	1½	2.4	Tolvan wood 2.40[c]	still there
BUFTON [4 Parcels]	[part of above]			Bufton Coppice 5.92	still there
TRENARTH The Wood		1	1.6		gone?
PONSAVERRION The Wood		½	0.8	0.96	still there
SECOMB WOLLAS The Wood		¾	1.2		gone
CALAMANSACK THE HIGHER The Woods [divided 11/12 and 1/12]		21	34.0	34.30[c]	still there
TRESAHER VEAN A Wood by Park Gilly		1	1.6	0.27	gone?
BUDOCK VEAN The Woods		1½	2.4		gone
TREBE WARTHA		1	1.6		gone

Table 2 Woods of Constantine in the 1649 survey and later.

a. Calculated on the basis the 21-foot perch was used in 1649.
b. Areas are decimalised from the 1841 measurements in (modern) acres, roods and perches.
c. Modern acreage of the wood as in 1841: the area entered on the tithe map is erroneous or incomplete.

approximately their present sizes. The rest was in seventeen groves of between 1 and 16 acres. Eleven of these small groves were still there in 1841 and seven are apparently still extant today.

Woods, fuel and the tin industry

The tin industry and its fuel

West Cornish tin was a major fuel-using industry in a very poorly wooded region. This was unusual: most heavy industries (e.g. the ironworks of the Weald) settled down in areas with plenty of woodland.

Although the famous Phœnician connexion is now discredited, Cornwall has been a major tin-producer for four thousand years, since the early Bronze Age.[52] In some places, owing to the previous destruction of woodland for farmland and moorland, wood fuel would already have been hard to come by from almost the beginning of the industry.

Cornwall, however, had many fuels. Furze and broom were abundant; they grew in many places, such as some of the slopes of the Helford River, that are now farmland or woodland. Most hamlets, such as Calamansack Wollas, had small commons usually including furze-ground. The geographer Carew in 1602 implies that furze was the chief domestic fuel of the county.[53] It was still used for baking within living memory on the Lizard Peninsula. In the tin industry it appears to have been used only in a first roasting of the ore to volatilise any arsenic.[54]

Peat was an important fuel, though not abundant or renewable: the deposits were thin and grew too slowly to be replaced after cutting. Most of the Lizard moors in air photographs show a pattern of fine curved striations, interspersed here and there with structures called 'hut-rectangles'; the latter are probably the sites of charcoal-hearths.[55] The thin blanket peat has at some time been pared away, partly for domestic fuel, partly to make charcoal for distant tinworks. Medieval grants, including the original Stannary Charter of 1201, often mention peat and peat charcoal as fuel.[56] Duchy of Cornwall estate accounts for Helston show considerable sums received for peat and peat charcoal in the fourteenth century, but almost none after 1422; this change, according to John Hatcher, points to the deposits around Helston being exhausted. Later

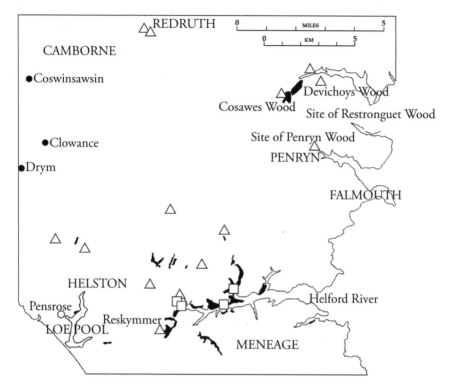

Fig. 3.5 Sites of blowing-houses (triangles) and limekilns (squares) in relation to ancient woodland (black) and sites of former woods (black spots). (DM 2018 after Rackham 1987.)

we find peat charcoal being brought to Cornwall from Dartmoor.[57] It was still used in Carew's time, but was later regarded as an inferior fuel.

Wood charcoal had been used by medieval tinworks as well as peat charcoal. From the fifteenth to the eighteenth century it was the chief fuel. Its use declined after an inventor in 1702 discovered how to smelt tin with mineral coal. Coal from South Wales was cheap, but for a long time tin smelted with it was thought to be inferior and liable to adulteration. (Nearly all the copper ore mined in West Cornwall was shipped to Wales to be smelted with coal.[58]) Some blowing-houses at St Austell used wood charcoal until the 1860s.[59]

How big was the tin industry and how much charcoal did it use? Tin, although rare, was not a particularly costly metal. In 1300, a pound of tin cost (to the English consumer) about 2.6*d.*, six times the price of a pound of iron. By 1700 the price of tin was around 7*d.* a pound, only three times the price of iron.[60] In real terms the price of tin had fallen by more than half in four hundred years.[61]

From 1300 to 1650, the production of tin in Cornwall had fluctuated around 600 tons per annum. In the late seventeenth century there was a steady increase, to around 1400 tons by 1700; the output further increased after the change to coal began, reaching 3500 tons by 1800. (Tin was taxed; these figures come from official records and thus do not include tin smuggled past the coinage-halls.)[62]

Over the centuries the centre of tin production moved westwards from Dartmoor to West Cornwall.[63] Though the Helston area was never the biggest producer, it had a long lifespan, with a peak probably in the seventeenth century. There was a big revival in the nineteenth century, but by then the tin was dug from deep mines and was almost certainly smelted with coal.

Tin was made from the ore in a small blast furnace in a blowing-house. Many such are known in the area, both from medieval records (from 1347 onwards) and from archaeological finds. The sites (Fig. 3.5) seem to be determined by streams (for driving the bellows) and by nearness to ore in streams and shallow deposits. In some instances (e.g. Reskymmer in Mawgan) nearness to a wood may have been a consideration, but most blowing-houses were well away from woodland. (At Bosahan the blowing-house is next to a wood, but the wood is probably younger.)

How much wood fuel was used? At a reasonable estimate, the production of tin with wood charcoal, within ten miles' radius of the Helford River woods, began at a few tens of tons a year in the early Middle Ages. It rose gradually (through increasing total production, and through the loss of peat as an alternative fuel) to a maximum of perhaps 150 tons in the mid-to-late-seventeenth century. It had probably ceased here by 1750.

In 1778, the mining writer Pryce said that a batch of ore yielded 8–12 hundredweight of tin by means of 18–24 packs of charcoal, each of 60 gallons.[64] Let us suppose that a gallon of charcoal was made from two gallons of stacked logs – about one-third of a cubic foot – which would contain about one-quarter of a cubic foot of solid wood, weighing roughly 8 pounds. On this basis, a ton of tin, 20 hundredweight, should have consumed on average 42 packs, that is 2500 gallons, of charcoal, representing 20,000 lb, or 10 tons, of wood.[65] Cornish woods probably grew at the rate of about one ton of wood per acre per year; this is a low estimate, but takes account of the severe exposure to wind and known slow growth at present (*see* page 93).

Tinning was thus not an enormous user of fuel. Iron-smelting at this late date used about 18 tons of wood to make a ton of iron but operated on a hundredfold larger scale. Both industries had probably learnt to economise on charcoal through gradual improvements to the design of furnaces.

At its peak in *c.*1700, the whole Cornish charcoal tin industry should have been using about 15,000 tons of wood a year, which ought to have been within the capacity of Cornish woodland. But there would have been social consequences, in that the tinners should have been able to outbid everyone else in the competition for the small wooded area. Already in 1602 Carew claimed that:

> the east quarters of the shire are not destitute of copsewoods, nor they of (almost) an intolerable price.

But Kerrier was less wooded than even the average for Cornwall. Here the industry, even in the early stages, was big enough to have consumed a sizeable proportion of the available supply of underwood. By Carew's time:

> their few parcels [of woodland] yet preserved are principally employed to [char]coaling, for blowing of tin. This lack [of domestic fuel] they supply either by stone coal fetched out of Wales, or by dried turfs ...

At its peak the Kerrier tin industry would have used up the entire wood production of the Helford River and other local woods, and more.

Accordingly in Kerrier, and even more in woodless Penwith, we find much evidence for the import of wood, charcoal, coal and timber. For example, in 1593 a cargo of 100 packs of charcoal and 30 small oaks went from Milford Haven to St Ives.[66] Charcoal came from Hampshire and Wales, timber from the Baltic and even Ireland. Gweek, in the midst of the Helford woods, was among the ports importing charcoal.[67, 68]

Fig. 3.6 Limekiln at Merthen Quay, September 2007.

Limekilns

The other fuel-using industry was burning lime for mortar and fertiliser.[69] In Kerrier lime was rare and limestone had to be shipped from a distance. Limekilns were sited at Merthen and Gweek where quays were near woods (Figs. 3.5, 3.6), although these would have been handy also for importing coal, which was the limeburners' preferred fuel.

Woodland management and industry

In 1530, there was again a dispute over Arundell Wood. It was agreed that even if John Skewys, lord of Merthen, was found to be the legal owner, he was to be given 'all such coles or the valew thereof as is colyd or cutt there'.[70] This implies that charcoal – the usual meaning of 'coal' in Cornwall unless stone-coal is specified – was already the normal product of the Helford River woods. The tinners, the only large-scale users of charcoal, had already secured the wood market.

The lessee of Tucoyse Wood, in 1604, was a local carpenter who was entitled:

> to fell, coal, and carry away the same, reserving ... all such standles as by the statute in that behalf are required to be left.[71]

This alludes to the statute of 1543, requiring 12 young timber-trees (here called standles) to be left on each acre of a wood every time it was felled. Such a clause occurs in wood-leases throughout England, although in south Cornwall it was usual to concentrate timber trees in one part of the wood instead of scattering them through the whole wood (*see* page 80).

In 1617 one of the Reskymmer family was given a yearly right to:

> half-a-waighe of Smith's coale yearly at All Saints' Day, to be delivered at the Weare in the easte wood of ... Merthen[72]

and also to ten packs of 'Charcke-Coale' from the manorial dues of bushellage; this implies that charcoal was being shipped out of Gweek port as well as in.

As we shall see, there is ample archaeological evidence for charcoal-burning from some of the woods but by no means all. Written evidence indicates that the woods were not of specially great value. The Merthen survey of *c.*1580 valued the standing trees at some 14s. per acre; a very low figure at the time,[73] considering that they would probably have been, on average, of at least ten years' growth since the last coppicing. The 1649 survey values all the woods in Constantine at 2s. 8d. per [big] acre per year, well below the then usual value of underwood in England, and well below the value attributed to arable and pasture (6–14s.).

The Calamansack Wood survey of *c.*1650 gives the price of £2 per acre for the standing wood: a more reasonable figure but by no means outstanding, given the probably long coppice rotation. Much of the value, however, was in the bark rather than the wood. Oak bark, sold for tanning, was a major by-product – later, sometimes the main product – of woodland in general.[74] Here, the high value set on bark, plus the fact that a valuation was set on pasture (a use of the wood which would have damaged its regrowth), show that even at this time of maximum demand charcoal was not the only consideration in managing the wood. Although the Helford River woods undoubtedly supplied charcoal to the tinworks, tinners had other sources of fuel and were not the only outlet for woodland produce.

Post-industrial woodsales

A run of woodsale books survives for Merthen and Calamansack Woods for various years from 1790 to 1825.[75] By this time charcoal was little used in the tinworks and none was made here. Wood was sold in the form of faggots and poles. For example, in the year 1820–1, in 'Kilmansack Wood', 9700 faggots were made and were sold to 58 named purchasers for £48 4s. 8d. 'Making and cleaning the wood' cost £15 15s. 3d.; 'carriing out of wood, Boat & Men in Boat' cost £9 8s. 8d.; leaving £25 3s. 11d. profit. Entries appear in the same form year by year, though the quantities vary: in 1789–90 Calamansack produced only 500 faggots, but in 1821–2 there were 14,700 sold to 142 buyers.

The woods had reverted to producing domestic fuel for sale to consumers, but were more profitable than they had been when tinworks had been using the wood as charcoal. In the 1820s, sales of faggots from Calamansack averaged £55 per annum; even though more than a third of this was spent on making the faggots, carrying, and men in boats, the net return came to £1 per acre per year, well above the average for woodland at the time.[76] Merthen appears to have brought in rather less for its size.

Cosawes Wood had an industrial use in the eighteenth century (*see* pages 111–2). In the middle was a gunpowder mill, presumably for making blasting powder for use in mines. It was probably put there for reasons of safety rather than supply: powder mills used charcoal of alder, of which there is little in or near the wood, although it could easily have been imported to the nearby Perran Wharf.

In Merthen Wood there are mentions of the 'first shred', 'fourth shred', etc as having been cut in different years. This might be taken to refer to the practice of shredding, cutting the side-boughs off a tree and leaving a tuft at the top;[77] but the wood today shows clearly that it has been coppiced normally since long before this period. The quantities of faggots sold leave no doubt that they were the main product. I conclude that the word 'shred' is merely an alternative to 'panel', 'hag', 'fell', 'cant', etc –

terms used in different parts of England for the area of underwood cut each year.

How much wood did the woods yield? In 1825 the Calamansack wood-sale took the form of 10 tons of 'Poles ... for fire Wood', value £8 10s. (less £1 5s. for 'Cutting and Carriing to the Water' and £1 5s. for 'Boat & Mens labour carring to different places'). This indicates that the retail price of wood was about 17s. per ton. A hundred faggots, which sold at 8s. or 10s., would thus have weighed roughly half a ton, allowing for the extra cost of labour in making them. In an average year (1821–5) Calamansack Wood produced 10,000 faggots, that is, 50 tons from 32 acres of woodland. This is rather more than would be expected from the very slow growth of the woods today, but faggots are an economical means of using twigs and boughs as well as big logs, and the five years for which we have figures may not be representative of the whole coppice cycle.

In both woods there were occasional small purchases of 'Binds' or 'Bonds' – the twistable rods of hazel (oak will not do) for tying up faggots. I infer that, then as now, some parts of Calamansack and Merthen Woods had enough hazel to bind the faggots, but in others there was no hazel, and bonds had to be bought.

There may have been a small revival of charcoal-burning: Henderson in the 1930s mentioned that some charcoal pits in Merthen Wood 'have been used within the memory of old people' – that is, c.1860.

In 1790 and 1791, the hedges of the woods were repaired at a cost of £5 8s. Maintaining boundaries, to keep out cattle and sheep which would eat the young shoots, was a chief expense of woodmanship throughout England.

There are a few references to 'weeding', both as an expense and as an income. In 1822–3, from Merthen, 2005 weedings were sold for £10 gross; each weeding was therefore a substantial pole selling at more than a penny. What exactly was being done is not clear. The Oxford English Dictionary gives several examples at around this date of the noun 'weeding', meaning a superfluous tree cut out of a wood or plantation – roughly equivalent to the present noun 'thinning'. In woods managed for bark, we hear recommendations to try to get rid of trees other than oak; but why should anyone have troubled to do this in a wood whose main product was fuel, for which the species hardly mattered?

Recent history

The woods get bigger

The woods of the Helford River have much increased since the seventeenth century, both naturally and as a result of planting.

Before the nineteenth century, woods are recorded sporadically on maps of estates (and on the Falmouth chart, *see* page 44). An eighteenth-century map of 'Helston Lake'[78] shows that the present Oak Grove[79] already existed as a thick wood-pasture-like scatter of trees, but the shores of the Loe Pool were otherwise woodless.

The earliest complete record of all but the smallest woods is the first Ordnance Survey: I shall quote from the draft survey of 1811[80] (Fig. 3.7), which differs slightly from the first publication of 1813. This is followed by the tithe maps and schedules of the various parishes, 1838–42;[83] and by the first edition 25-inch OS, surveyed 1876–8, the second edition, 1906, the partial third edition, 1933, and the fourth edition, 1973–4.

Many of the present plantations and a little of the natural secondary woodland arose in the late eighteenth and early nineteenth centuries and are there on the 1811 map. Most of the early plantations were on the south side of the Helford River, on the Trelowarren and Penrose estates.[81] The magnificent beeches at Trelowarren itself are dated, on the evidence of annual rings, to 1779. Most of the plantations, including those on the plateau south of the house, appear to be a little later, but are nearly all there on the 1811 map. There is much truth in the claim that Sir Vyell Vyvyan created the present richly tree'd appearance of Trelowarren.[82] Merthen North Wood must date from very soon after 1811: it looks like an abortive plantation which turned into a semi-natural wood. The beech grove between the Tremayne Woods is a successful plantation of the same date.

The tithe maps of *c.*1840 show the ancient woods almost exactly as they are now. Most of the plantations were already in place and are recorded as such, though there was occasional hesitation as to what was wood and what was plantation. For instance, Gwarth-an-drea Plantation is scheduled as 'Plantation', in contrast to Gweek Wood adjacent, which is 'Wood'; but Halliggye Plantation is called 'Wood or Plantation'. On the north side of the Helford, a group of plantations had appeared on Porthnavas Creek opposite Calamansack Wood.[83]

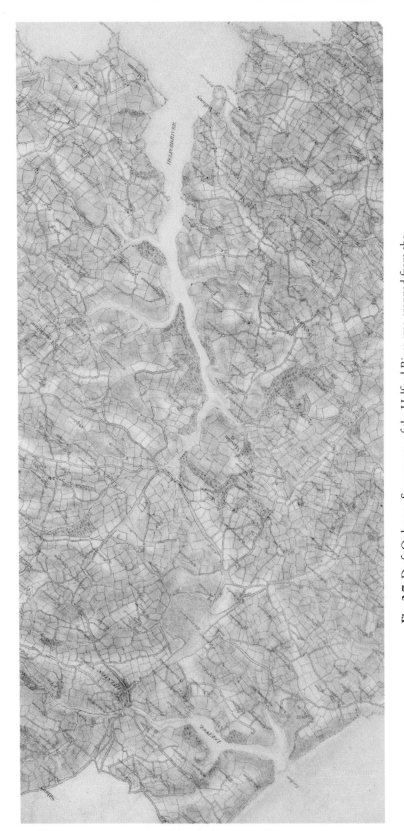

Fig. 3.7 Draft Ordnance Survey map of the Helford River area cropped from the Helston area map 1811 from Wikimedia.org and National Archives under the Open Government Licence. The labels on the map are canted at 45 degrees because the original is angled north-west/south-east and the crop has been rotated.

The 1811 Ordnance Survey shows Devichoys Wood much bigger than it is now, extending a mile and more to the east to mingle with the woods around the country-house park of Carclew. This appears on a larger scale on the tithe map of Mylor parish, 1842, which schedules the extensions as 'Plantation' and depicts them with a mixture of conifer and broadleaved symbols, unlike Devichoys Wood itself which has broadleaved only.[84]

In the 1840s, natural secondary woodland was still in a minority. Most such woods are on sites recorded on the tithe maps as pasture, furze, or orchard. Their development can be followed in the successive Ordnance Surveys. An example is between Bonallack and Merthen Woods, a steep hillside which had been the site of the medieval Arundell Wood (*see* page 158, Fig. AM1). On the 1842 map this area was all fields, except for a strip still called Arndle Wood (mentioned in the 1791 Merthen wood-book) adjoining Merthen West Wood. The 1877 map shows that the fields to the west, in the ravine adjoining Bonallack Wood, had become wooded. By 1906 there was a further wooded area and more of the land still has become woodland since. Such a story could be told of steep valleys and river edges throughout the area.

Declining management

Most of the ancient coppice-woods fell out of use, at widely differing dates: several woods were last felled as long ago as the 1820s. Few, if any, of the secondary woods were brought into management. Bonallack Wood was probably the only one to be regularly felled into the mid-twentieth century. The Ordnance Survey makes desultory attempts to show the state of coppicing by varying the kind of tree symbols used (e.g. Bonallack Wood 1906) or even by representing a felled area with 'rough grass' symbols (Polglase Wood 1906).

The destructions of ancient woodland for agriculture in the 1850s and 1860s and again a hundred years later, which affected so many English landscapes, almost passed by these woods. There were some grubbings, unfashionably, in the late nineteenth century: Grambla Wood and one of the Tolvan groves. Much of the rest of Grambla was grubbed in the 1970s.

Among the plantations, only the more accessible ones have fulfilled their destiny of being felled for timber and replanted (e.g. those south of Trelowarren at least once). Other plantations fell into disuse and have turned into some approximation of natural woodland. Most of the plantations adjoining Devichoys Wood were grubbed between 1930 and 1958.

From Georgian times trees have been planted in existing woods, with varying degrees of success. Most replantings involved at least some conifers and can thus be traced through conifer symbols on Ordnance maps. Replanting became a fashion which, as we have seen, reached its height in East Cornwall in the 1950s and 1960s. Big woods tended not to escape; for example, Three Lords' Wood north of Truro, which Charles Henderson thought was 'the Forest of Moroys ... where Tristan hid with Iseult' was a victim.

The Helford River escaped the excesses of the fashion: most replanting was of previous plantations. Where it did affect ancient woods, replanting often has not succeeded. The following seems to be a complete list:

Trelowarren Mills Wood: drastically replanted with beech and fir (*Abies*) *c.*1800.

Tremayne Little Wood: drastically planted with beech in the early nineteenth century.

Carminowe Wood: a few pine, beech, sycamore survive from before 1877.

Treverry Wood: a patch of conifers introduced before 1877.

Trelowarren Wood: conifers introduced in parts in the mid-nineteenth century; upper slopes severely replanted *c.*1950.

Gweek Wood: light replanting before 1877 (of which a few conifers survive); about half the wood drastically replanted *c.*1960.

Polwheveral Wood: a little planting in the late nineteenth century, of which a few beech and Turkey Oak survive.

Bosahan Wood: drastically and successfully replanted with beech *c.*1900; very little of previous wood survives.

Merthen Wood: small part has conifer symbols on OS 1906 map; few planted trees now survive.

Bufton Wood: some conifer symbols on OS 1906; no planted trees survive.

Reskymmer Wood: most of wood severely replanted in the 1960s but now recovering.

Urbanisation

The last big change in the landscape came to Porthnavas Creek in the 1930s. Land was sold in plots for building bungalows and chalets – a development akin to the more genteel parts of the plotland of South Essex.[85] This seldom involved ancient woods, but houses did eat up part of Tregithey Wood, as well as the prehistoric round outside. In the same spirit about two acres of Calamansack Wood were grubbed out to build a large holiday house and two cottages. Fifty years on, Porthnavas Creek still looks very un-Cornish, with its ill-assorted modern houses, incongruous gardens and huge exotic trees such as *Pinus radiata*. Many of the larger plots have been invaded by sycamore to form secondary woodland.

Coppicing never entirely fell out of use; the practice was kept alive in Bonallack Wood. In the last ten years there has been a revival.

Grey squirrel arrived *c.*1965.[86]

The great storms of 1987 and 1990 had only very local effects on the ancient woods, despite the havoc wrought among great beeches and *Pinus radiata* outside woods. The storm affected mostly very tall trees in situations sheltered from ordinary winds, as in the timberwood part of Calamansack Wood.

Merthen and other woods are said to have been used, improperly, in the twentieth century for wintering cattle.

There seems to have been only a small amount of shooting in the woods. The principal sport was shooting woodcock, which here came on migration and did not breed. Woodcock have the reputation of being a difficult and sporting bird to hit. Before the coming of sporting guns, 'cockshooting' consisted of catching woodcock in a net strung across a narrow 'cockglade' between two parts of a wood; I cannot say whether this ever happened in Cornwall.

4 Archaeology

Boundaries and woodbanks

Most ancient woods are surrounded by a great earthwork, a *woodbank*, typically with a ditch on the outside. Many woodbanks are of medieval or earlier date. In stone country, woodbanks may be revetted with a dry-stone facing on the outside, often added later.[47] Woods were valuable: boundaries and security played a big part in their history.

The Helford River woods have boundary earthworks consisting of a bank and ditch, or a drystone wall, or both combined. Like most ancient wood boundaries, these do not run in straight lines but are sinuous or zigzag. They vary greatly in size and character, even within the same wood, and were evidently made piecemeal over a long period. Even such a tiny wood as Tolvan-Wollas has been quite massively embanked, which shows that at one time it was a valuable asset. The sea frontages lack earthworks. When a wood ends along a stream (e.g. Trelowarren Mills Wood), there is normally a wall excluding the stream from the wood.

The greatest of the woodbanks is one stretch of the perimeter of Carminowe Wood, with a bank and ditch 38 ft [11.58 m] in total width. The rest of the boundary is less remarkable; probably the wood was once much bigger and retains only part of its original margin. Calamansack Wood (Fig. 4.1) has massive revetted banks on all the land sides, especially on the north and west; the northern earthwork is 29 ft [8.84 m] wide including the ditch. Tremayne Great and Little Woods, in part, are almost as strongly enclosed (Fig. 4.2); the revetting of Great Wood is of regular stones and may have been added to the bank by the Vyvyans in the eighteenth century. Reskymmer Wood has a strong woodbank only on the south-east side, where it adjoined a meadow

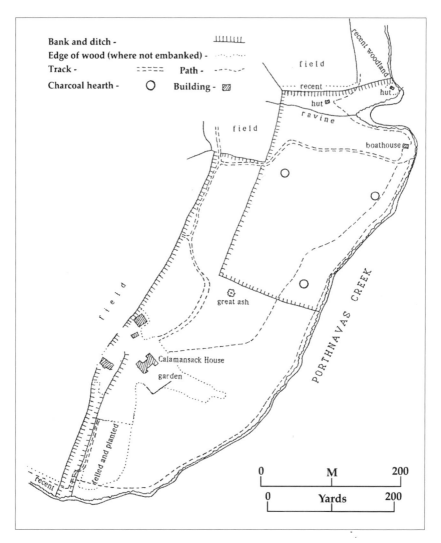

Fig. 4.1 Calamansack Wood – Topography and earthworks.

and the boundary would have been particularly important. Bonallack Wood, although a well-documented medieval wood, has comparatively weak banks, except in the ravine on the east side where a massive wall divides it from the former Arundell Wood (Fig. AM1). Merthen has somewhat miscellaneous walls and banks, the strongest (32 ft [9.75 m]) being on part of the north side of East Wood.

Fig. 4.2 Tremayne Little Wood western boundary bank running down to the Helford River, September 2018 (photograph by P. Holley).

Internal boundaries

Calamansack Wood is divided by an earthen bank and ditch, 19 ft [5.79 m] wide, which runs in nearly straight lines and is therefore relatively late (Fig. 4.1). It divides the wood approximately two-thirds and one-third, and thus corresponds to the division of the manor recorded in 1573. In the west of the wood there is a sinuous, low, probably earlier, bank of uncertain meaning.

Merthen East and West Woods are divided by a wall along the middle stream (which belongs to East Wood). East Wood is further divided by other walls and by a lane (*see* Fig. 4.3). A similar streamside wall divides Trelowarren Wood. There is a strong bank bisecting the original part of Grambla Wood.

Relation to hillforts and rounds

Wood boundaries can incorporate earlier earthworks. Part of the perimeter of Tremayne Great and Little Woods has a kind of flat-bottomed ditch, like a holloway, just outside the woodbank. This appears to extend beyond the woods, continued by the edges of fields and plantations, and may once have formed a complete circuit (*see* page 162, Fig. AM5). The earlier Ordnance Survey editions show this feature, incompletely, as an ancient 'Camp'. Possibly it formed an outer enceinte to the structure, supposed to have been an Iron Age round, which stood until recently in the middle of it. The thought of it as a Roman camp doubtless inspired the spelling 'Vallum Tremayne Creek' for the arm of the Helford River alongside. The tithe map spells this, probably correctly, as 'Vellan Tremayne', meaning Tremayne Mill.

A similar earthwork borders Merthen North and part of East Wood, and may have stood in the same relation to the square 'round' in the middle. A third borders Trelowarren Wood. The Ordnance Survey maps similar outworks to Gear and Caervallack, which today form the boundaries of recent woodland below these hillforts.

The Trelowarren earthwork is mapped by the OS as an antiquity, 'Park Pale'. This may indeed have been its function – it would be in just the place, below the edge of the plateau, for a 'ha-ha' or hidden fence to a landscape park.[87] A park explanation, as we have seen, is also possible at Merthen, and is conceivable at Tremayne, though hardly at Gear or Caervallack.

I conclude that where an Iron Age round or hillfort was on the high point of a plateau, it commonly had an outer earthwork at the break of the slope. This could have defined the top edge of whatever woodland may then have clothed the slope. The outer earthwork later served as a medieval woodbank, or as the perimeter of a park on the plateau, or as the top edge of a post-medieval wood. On this theory there could be yet another round, now lost, at Trelowarren.

Lanes and tracks

Merthen Wood is traversed by three ancient holloways down to the shore. The principal one is all that remains of a road from Constantine church-town to Merthen quay. This narrow, deeply sunk lane (Fig. 4.3), probably only for packhorse traffic, is divided by woodbanks from the wood on either side. Other holloways descend to the pills in the east and west of the wood. These were evidently private ways, and are not demarcated from the wood. The western one zigzags deep and headlong through Arundell Wood: this, rather than the present quay in Bonallack Wood, seems to have been Bonallack hamlet's access to the sea. A small

Fig. 4.3 Principal holloway in Merthen Wood, September 2007.

holloway descends to the pill in Tremayne Little Wood.

Adjacent to Carminowe Wood is a deep holloway, a fragment of a through road, truncated only a century ago.

Many of the woods have well-constructed tracks through them. These are of unknown date, and were evidently intended for carting out wood or charcoal. Such a track, for example, traverses the otherwise very steep Tregithey Wood, and there are others in Carminowe, Grambla, and even the little Tolvan-Wartha Wood.

The main road through Gweek Wood, unusually for a road in an ancient wood, is not demarcated by banks. This is because the road is modern, originally made as the private drive to Trelowarren, and has only recently become a public highway.

Charcoal-hearths

Charcoal is made by allowing wood to smoulder in an insufficient supply of air. An ancient method, evidently used here, is to make a closely packed circular stack of logs, cover it with bracken and earth, ignite it from within, and watch it carefully while it cooks itself during a week or so. Charcoal-hearth sites can now be found as level circular platforms scooped into the hillside, some 30 ft [9 m] in diameter. Under the leaf mould they are thickly strewn with pieces of charcoal, among which, so far, I have identified only oak.

Charcoal-hearths are common in the northern woods. I have found them in Grambla, Bonallack and Calamansack Woods; there are at least three in the small Polwheveral Wood. Henderson reported them 'all over Merthen Woods', but these are now hidden. In the southern woods I have found them only in Carminowe and Tregithey. They are likely to have been most active in the seventeenth century.

Quays

Merthen Quay (Fig. 4.4), known as Merthen Hole, was once a small port; it was probably still in use at the time of the 1877 map. Fifty years later, Charles Henderson wrote in his *Parish of Constantine* (1937):

> On the shore of Gweek river ... is an old Quay, known as Merthen Hole. This is approached by a deeply sunk pack-horse track ... over the Downs to Brill. Near the Quay is a ruined limekiln, and by its side a cottage, which was burnt many years ago. The foundations of a small circular building near the Quay are possibly those of a kiln for burning kelp. Close by is a small creek ... On the edge of this is a large rectangular pit in which are three graves, said to be those of sailors who died of some contagious disease.[88]

Fig. 4.4 Merthen Quay from Tremayne Wood, September 2007.

Fig. 4.5 Quarry at sea edge of Bonallack Wood, September 2007.

Sixty years' more trees and bushes have grown up since then, but the quay still stands, built of mighty granite blocks, as do the limekiln and ruined cottage; the pit is still there, though the graves are not discernible.

Remains of smaller quays can be seen in most of the woodland pills (e.g. in Calamansack Wood), though the present boathouses are sited elsewhere. Most of the quays have access for horses but not carts; they may therefore date from the post-medieval period, when vehicles seem to have gone out of general use in Cornwall. At Tremayne Little Wood is the quay (with a built-up road to it through Great Wood), built in the hope of a visit by Queen Victoria.

Industrial remains

A mill-leat runs through Trelowarren Mills Wood and another through the recent woods in the Vellan Tremayne valley. Bosahan Wood is traversed by a leat supplying a huge, but apparently unrecorded, water-wheel. Also in this wood are the remains of a blowing-house.

Several of the woods contain small pits and quarries. An old mine-shaft is recorded next to Bufton Wood. In Bonallack Wood there is a sizeable quarry, accessible only from the sea (Fig. 4.5).

5 Flora

Plant life varies widely from one wood to another, depending on the wood's history, its management and soils, and other influences more difficult to discover. Most ancient woods are rich in plant species, including rarities. The number of species depends, among other factors, on the size of the wood, but not in any simple way: other things being equal, a wood of five times the area will have about twice the flora.[89]

On the Helford River the wood with the most species of native flowering plants and ferns[90] is Merthen, which is by far the biggest wood. The outstandingly rich wood for its size is Trelowarren Wood, doubtless because of its very varied soils.

As a group, the Helford River woods are among the richer ancient woods in England in their flowering plants and ferns. Except for Trelowarren Wood, they are less outstanding in their variety of trees and shrubs: some English trees do not reach this remote corner of Cornwall. Trelowarren Mills Wood and Tremayne Little Wood are much poorer (for their size) than the others, probably because of their drastic replanting long ago.

Oaks

The common oak of England is the 'pedunculate' species, *Quercus robur*, which grows as timber trees in woods of other species, in wood-pasture, hedges, recent woods, alongside railways, indeed everywhere except oak-dominated woods. Sessile oak, *Q. petraea*, is the special oak of oakwoods; rare in eastern England, it increases westwards until in West Cornwall (except the Lizard) it is abundant in the landscape generally, not just in woodland.

Most of the Helford River woods are composed of sessile oak (Fig. 5.1). The northern woods are particularly good examples of sessile oakwood,

Fig. 5.1 Sessile oak in Tremayne Woods, April 2016 (photograph by G. F. Peterken).

with barely any detectable admixture or hybridisation of the common species. On the Lizard Peninsula most oaks are pedunculate, and this species occurs in some of the southern Helford woods, as well as in the non-wooded landscape.

Both oaks are very variable when they occur as wild trees; hence subtly varied colours of the canopy of these woods, especially in early autumn as individual trees develop different colours, some earlier than others. A variant that deserves mention is sessile oak with very shallowly lobed leaves, common in and around Merthen Wood and in Cosawes Wood.

When people plant oaks, they tend to select acorns from trees that they think will produce good timber; the resulting trees tend to be all much the same. As far as I can tell, there has been little planting of oak in these woods, and I have not recorded any stands of plantation-type oaks. This matters, because wild-type oaks, with their crooked trunks and prodigious spreading boughs, are part of the landscape character, the *genius loci*, of Cornwall. Moreover, they are the host to the epiphytes – polypody and other ferns, wood sorrel, and many bryophytes – that form ecosystems of their own with accumulated leaf mould and the animals that live in it; these are the last northern outlier of the massive 'fern-gardens' high in the trees of tropical rainforests.[91]

Elms

Woodland elms are rare but of interest, like all elms in Cornwall. The elms of farmsteads and (mostly recent) groves throughout West Cornwall are of three kinds, all of which may be early introductions: the Cornish Elm and its relative the 'Lizard' elm, members of the *Ulmus stricta* group of elms; and the 'Dutch' Elm, probably a hybrid between wych-elm (*U. glabra*) and one of the East Anglian (*U. minor*) group of elms.[92] These country elms have suckered into the edges of several of the woods, but otherwise do not occur in ancient woodland at all.

Wych-elm itself is very rare in Cornwall – the many authors who state the contrary have confused it with Dutch Elm. In Trelowarren Wood are scattered coppice stools of an elm which (though showing some signs of past hybridisation with a *stricta* elm) is probably the nearest approximation to wych-elm so far found native in West Cornwall. Its status is open to the same questions as that of lime but, since lime and wych-elm are found together in one of the few places where the soils are suitable for them, I incline to the view that both are native. Real wych-elm also occurs at the south-west corner of Merthen West Wood, but only on the woodbank; it may have been planted to define the boundary.

A somewhat similar elm, but with more Cornish Elm characters, forms a large clone in Tremayne Great Wood: it combines the big leaves of *glabra* with the upright shape and suckering habit of *stricta*.

Lime – the mysterious tree

The native lime, *Tilia cordata*, is another most important historic tree, a living link with the wildwood (*see* page 32), and now uncommon and almost confined to ancient woodland. In Cornwall there are, as

Fig. 5.2 Lime stool in Trelowarren Wood, September 2007.

everywhere else, many planted trees of *Tilia vulgaris*, the tree-planters' lime, which is a hybrid between *T. cordata* and *T. platyphyllos*, the other species of native lime. Native lime is rare in the Highland Zone (*see* page 32) and hitherto has been thought to be absent from Cornwall: the nearest known to me is in Holne Chase, a wood on the other side of Dartmoor.

There are, however, limes in some of these woods. In Trelowarren Wood there are four stools varying somewhat between *cordata* and *platyphyllos*, with leaves of *cordata* shape but bigger and hairier like *platyphyllos* (Fig. 5.2). Ordinarily, these would be accepted as relics of wildwood, but Trelowarren Wood belonged to the Vyvyans, a notable tree-planting family, and contains non-indigenous trees, such as beeches and horse chestnuts, which they must have introduced. However, their planted limes are nearly always clearly recognisable as *T. vulgaris*. Three of the limes are big coppice stools, 5 to 7 ft [1.5–2.13 m] in diameter, and are therefore likely to be older than any of the Vyvyans' plantings, and much older than the other planted trees in the wood. They are not the same as any of the ordinary forms of *vulgaris*, nor are they identical to each other, which planted limes, derived from suckers from the same tree, ought to be.

The matter is complicated by the discovery of a huge lime stool, 8½ ft [2.59 m] in diameter, similar to the Trelowarren Wood limes, in Reskymmer Wood, which has no parkland connexion. Three more turned up, far to the west, in the oakwood of Nance Wood; these are more typical of *cordata*. One *Tilia cordata* is reported from the cliff edge near Helford.[93]

From this I infer that lime – as the pollen record shows (*see* pages 32–3) – had its outliers in the wildwood of Cornwall, as in that of Wales; and, being very difficult to destroy, a few stools persist to this day.

Exotic trees and shrubs

Sycamore is a tree from the north side of the mountains in Central Europe. It became a popular garden tree in the seventeenth century, despite the disapproval of John Evelyn the dendrologist. Several of the early records, from 1635 onwards, refer to Cornwall,[94] whose damp, windy climate reminds it of its homeland. It flourishes even though the woodland soils might be thought rather infertile for it.

Sycamore is recorded from almost all the West Cornwall woods. Rarely have I found big coppice stools (Tremayne Little Wood, 9 ft diameter [2.74 m]) which might date from near the original introduction. More often it occurs as single-stemmed trees or trees that have been felled only once. There was evidently a phase of increase, partly by planting but mostly by seeding from trees planted outside the woods, around the time the woods ceased to be coppiced.

Beech, though native in the New Forest and south-east Wales, appears to be an introduction in Cornwall. Nowhere have I seen the ancient pollards that are, or were, a feature of most native beech localities. It was evidently a fashionable tree in the late eighteenth century; within the woods are a very few huge, old, now veteran beeches that date from around that time. Beech follows the rise of the practice of planting within existing woods, although most post-1950 beeches have been ruined as timber by the bite of rabbits and grey squirrels.

Beech tends to spread because, like sycamore, the young trees tolerate shade and will grow under the canopy of oak. It is more wind-resistant than oak and tends to project through the oak canopy.[95, 96]

Turkey Oak (*Quercus cerris*) is said to have been first introduced from south-east France in 1735 by William Lucombe I, Exeter nurseryman.[97] It had a brief period of being a fashionable tree in the early twentieth century, when foresters wanted to grow oak but were beginning to be obsessed with fast growth. The timber was unsaleable, but the tree persisted. Although present in about half the West Cornwall woods it is, as yet, not abundant.

Sweet chestnut in the rest of England is an archaeophyte, introduced from an unknown origin in the Roman period, and now forming giant stools and entering into ancient woodland as if it were a native. In West Cornwall, however, it is a much more recent introduction, occurring only as single stems or as stools cut just once and not spreading. It appears to have been introduced in the planting phase of the late nineteenth century.

Rhododendron was originally an exotic, a rare plant from either Portugal or the Black Sea, introduced *c.*1780 and highly fashionable in the nineteenth century for its pretty flowers.[98, 99] Whether the Cornish plant is really the original *Rhododendron ponticum*, or what is in effect a new species created by allowing it to hybridise with the American *Rh.*

catawbiense,[100] has yet to be found out. It has taken over many woods (almost exclusively oakwoods), killing everything else through the chemicals that it secretes. Here it is rather local, except in Devichoys Wood where much effort has been put into getting rid of it.

Giant Fir, *Abies grandis*, was discovered in 1825 in the Pacific rainforest of North America. It was a favourite tree of Victorian planters. Its ragged, lightning-strike outline, towering above all other trees, still signals many a Victorian park. There are a few magnificent old trees in Gweek and Trelowarren woods. Unlike the preceding trees it shows no inclination to spread.

Rare and uncommon plants and species of ancient woodland

Service, *Sorbus torminalis*, another rare tree, is scattered along the coastal fringes of the northern Helford River woods (Fig. 5.3), with one locality south of the river, on the cliff edge near Helford.[101] This is one of those plant species that are associated with ancient woods.[102] It is otherwise almost unknown in Cornwall; as far as is known it has no Cornish name. The services in Gweek Wood are the westernmost outside Portugal. Service here is nearly always a small tree. It is weakly clonal: the biggest patch is in Bonallack Wood, 59 ft [18 m] across. Its leaves are attacked by a special gall insect, *Eriophyes torminalis*. Trelowarren Wood has several other rare and uncommon woodland plants: tutsan *Hypericum androsaemum*, Solomon's Seal *Polygonatum multiflorum* (probably its only native locality in Cornwall), and one of the two Lizard records of orpine *Sedum telephium* – the only succulent plant that grows in woods (Fig. 5.4). For its size, Trelowarren is the richest of these woods in those plants that go with ancient woodland. Merthen Wood is probably the only locality in West Cornwall for alder buckthorn *Frangula alnus*. It has that Cornish speciality bastard-balm *Melittis melissophyllum* – the most beautiful of all the deadnettle relatives in Britain – and also columbine *Aquilegia vulgaris* and tutsan. Species uncommon in this part of England include skullcap *Scutellaria galericulata* and the fern *Polystichum setiferum*.[103] Several clifftop and saltmarsh plants are an unusual addition to the flora of this wood.

In the recent woods of Vellan Tremayne the rare leek *Allium babingtonii*, though not traditionally regarded as a woodland plant, is

Fig. 5.3 Service tree on the edge of Bonallack Wood, September 2007.

Fig. 5.4 *Sedum telephium*, Trelowarren Wood, June 1980.

rapidly expanding. Columbine also grows there. Royal fern *Osmunda regalis* grows in several of the damp valleys. Herbaceous plants have responded to the custom that gardeners, in the nineteenth and much of the twentieth century, made it a point of honour not to grow native plants. If they wanted yellow archangel it must not be the beautiful native plant, *Lamiastrum galeobdolon ssp. montanum*, but a variegated lookalike of unknown origin, *Lamiastrum galeobdolon ssp. argentatum*. They would find out too late that variegated archangel is a highly aggressive plant: if you let it into your garden you soon find yourself growing nothing else. I am dismayed to have recorded *argentatum* in four woods but *montanum* only once.

Mosses, liverworts and lichens

The only wood studied in detail is Trelowarren Mills, where mosses and liverworts were thoroughly recorded from 1962 to 1971. There is a long list (100 species), including two national rarities and several other scarce species. The liverwort *Dumortiera hirsuta* is predominantly

Fig. 5.5 *Hookeria lucens* (photograph by H. Schachner).

tropical, and is known in only one other place in Cornwall. The moss *Ditrichum subulatum* is recorded only in Cornwall, Devon and Kent. This wood is (or was then) a first-class locality for bryophytes, and probably also for lichens, from its sheltered situation in a damp north-facing valley well away from acid rain, and from the mouldering trunks of giant trees fallen during many years' lack of management. The rare and elusive filmy-fern *Hymenophyllum tunbridgense* might yet be found in such a place.

Some of the other south Helford River woods may also be good, though they are probably too well looked-after to be first-class: tidiness is death to these plants. The northern woods, though well supplied with bryophytes and lichens, are probably less outstanding: they are relatively dry, and may in the past have been fumigated by tin and arsenic works not far away. The rare moss *Fissidens curnowii* and the strongly oceanic *Hookeria lucens* (Fig. 5.5) have been recorded.[104]

6 Vegetation

This chapter is concerned with vegetation, the trees and other plants in terms of their abundance and their relation to other species.

Woods consist of trees and shrubs; herbaceous plants and undershrubs (e.g. brambles, heather); epiphytes (mosses and liverworts, lichens, polypody fern) growing on the trees; and mosses and liverworts on rocks or soil. Some authorities, such as the National Vegetation Classification, try to classify woods on the basis that trees and shrubs form integrated plant communities with the ground vegetation (herbs + undershrubs) and maybe ground-living mosses and lichens. In practice, trees often change, for example in going down a slope, with no change in the ground vegetation, and vice versa. Hence I take the view that trees and shrubs form one set of plant communities. They form part of the environment for a separate set of plant communities of herbs and undershrubs.

The trees

Structure of the woods

In the main these are oakwoods. Sessile oak is greatly predominant; it forms both the underwood (*see* page 25) and the timber trees, if any. Only locally do other trees form the canopy. Although thus composed, for long stretches, of only one tree, these woods are not monotonous: it is characteristic of ancient oakwoods that the trees vary enormously in size and shape. Full-grown oak trees, within the same wood, can be anything from 5 to 90 ft [1.5–27.43 m] high.

The ancient woods are, or have been, coppices; the oaks have several stems from a common base. They vary widely in age since last felling. Bonallack Wood was cut partly in 1962 and partly in 1944; Trelowarren Wood *c.*1950; Tremayne Great Wood (as shown by annual rings) in

Fig. 6.1 Ancient sessile oak stool in Bonallack Wood, September 2007.

1921; Merthen and Calamansack Woods (from annual rings) partly in the 1820s and partly more recently, down to the 1930s; several other woods well back in the nineteenth century.

The woods, like most ancient woods, are not in places good for growing trees. There has been so little felling that it has not been easy to find annual rings to count. Growth is variable, though usually slow: it is very difficult to estimate the year's growth of a stool by looking at it. A normal pattern is for growth to be moderately slow for sixty to eighty years, and then so very slow that the rings are difficult to count and are probably underestimated. The oldest stems that I found were two oaks, of *c.*1715 and *c.*1760, blown down in the 1990 storm in the ravine of Calamansack Wood.

Although, as we have seen, most of the historical records are of underwood, there are a few references to timber trees. In the normal 'coppice-with-standards' woods of England it is usual for the standard (timber) trees to be scattered among the coppice stools. On the Helford River it was evidently the practice to grow timber trees all together in a sheltered ravine (for which I shall use the Irish term *timberwood*).

79

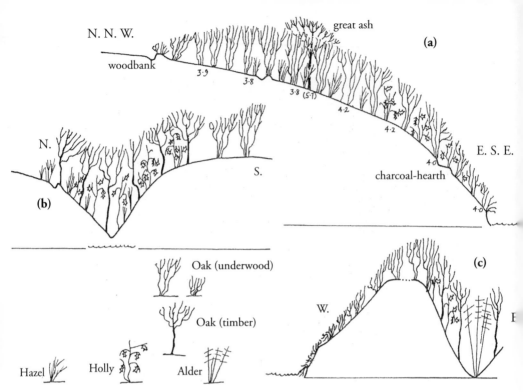

Fig. 6.2 Profiles of woods (a) across middle of Calamansack Wood, at right angles to slope – numbers are measurements of soil pH; (b) across northern ravine of Calamansack Wood; (c) across peninsula of Merthen Wood, just west of Middle Pill. Twofold vertical exaggeration.

The eastern valley of Bonallack Wood and the northern valley of Calamansack (Fig. 6.2b) are full of great oaks, with little or no sign of coppicing, and have a sharp boundary with the coppiced wood. The upper slopes in the three valleys of Merthen Wood are similar (Fig. 6.2c). The little Tolvan-Wollas Wood and Tregithey Wood are each divided into a timberwood and a coppice; there are possible traces of the practice in Tremayne Great Wood and Gweek Wood. Separating timber and underwood was no doubt essential here, since oaks would not grow to timber shape on the exposed slopes; but even where this was not a consideration, the Helford practice ought to have been to the benefit of both modes of growing the trees, and it is surprising that it should not have been adopted elsewhere. (A few of the inland woods appear to have been conventional coppice-with-standards.)

As in most ancient woods the stools vary in size, and include giants resulting from many cycles of felling and regrowth. Stools measuring

5 ft [1.5 m] in diameter and several hundred years old are common in most of the woods. Oak stools 10 ft [3.05 m] in diameter were noted in Calamansack Wood, and one of 14 ft [4.27 m] in Merthen East Wood. Such giant stools are one of the most distinctive features of ancient woods (Fig. 6.1).

The oaks are of the twisted, corkscrew shape which is normal in Cornwall. They show genetic variation in such things as burrs and twigs on the trunk, degree of crookedness, and times of leaf-opening and of leaf-fall. This variation is the cause of the mottled greens of the woodland canopy as seen from a distance. We can recognise oaks as individuals, and can decide whether a group of stems comprises one stool or more than one.

Wind exposure evidently determines the height of the oaks. It halts their upward growth or deflects them sideways. Uprooting – the effect of wind that most concerns modern foresters – or breakage seldom occur. Gales probably take effect by depositing salt spray on tender shoots: oaks appear to be more susceptible to salt than most trees. The most stunted trees are exposed either to easterly winds (e.g. the point

Fig. 6.3 Dwarf oak on edge of Gweek Wood, September 2007.

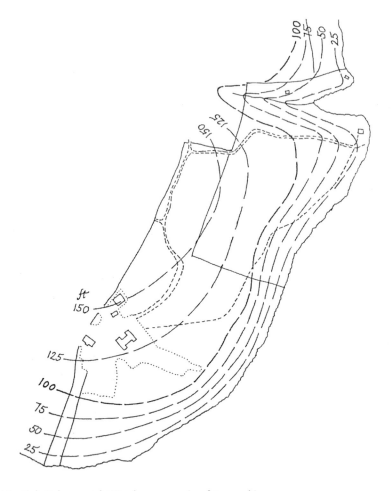

Fig. 6.4 Calamansack Wood: contours (25-ft intervals).

of Gweek Wood, Fig. 6.3) or to westerly (the west side of the middle point of Merthen Wood). Local funnelling and sheltering are evidently important. Trees tend to be higher in the middle of a wood than at the edges (Fig. 6.2a). The canopy forms a smoothly sculptured surface, which does not follow the shape of the hill underneath.

Tremayne Little Wood and Trelowarren Mills Wood were so drastically replanted long ago that they have lost most of their structure as woodland. The latter wood, when I visited it in 1970–1, was a long-neglected plantation, with immense oaks, ashes, beeches, firs and sycamores, and full of dead or fallen trees mantled in moisture-loving

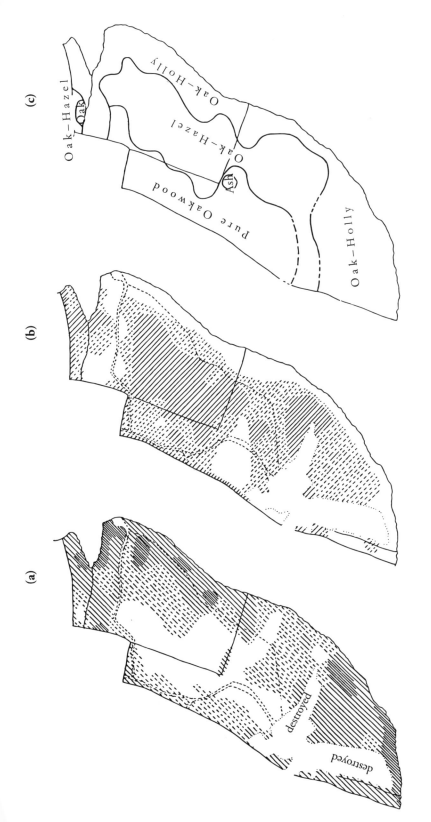

Fig. 6.5 Calamansack Wood: distribution of (a) holly, (b) hazel and (c) tree communities.

mosses; it gave an illusion of wildwood now rarely seen.

There are two surviving examples of wood-pasture, with large, non-coppice oaks scattered in grassland or heath. There are signs of possible pollarding among the old oaks of Oak Grove, Penrose.

Types of woodland

This is an account of the natural vegetation of the long-established woods; I pass over, for the moment, recent woodland and woods which have been so successfully replanted that the original trees can no longer be recognised. I deal separately with the plant communities formed by the trees and shrubs on the one hand, and the herbaceous plants and undershrubs on the other; sometimes there is a correlation between the two, but often the ground vegetation changes with no corresponding change in the trees.

These woods are typically Cornish in their variation on a limited number of tree species. Oakwoods, which predominate, can be divided into pure oakwood, oak–hazel, and oak–holly. There are five other tree communities in which oak is not dominant. Table 3 summarises the occurrence of the eight tree communities.

In pure oakwood, oak is the only tree except for rare individuals of service, rowan, holly and (recently introduced) beech. This kind of woodland predominates in all the northern coastal woods from Gweek to Calamansack. It is the woodland of the least fertile soils, on which only oak and a few other very undemanding trees will grow; it occurs most consistently on the plateau, from which minerals have been leached away.

In oak–holly wood, holly is abundant, and may form continuous thickets beneath the oak (Fig. 6.6). Oak–holly is extensive in Calamansack Wood, best developed on the lower slopes (Figs. 6.2a, 6.5); it probably indicates less infertile, though still acidic, soils. It occurs widely in Merthen and Bonallack Woods, impressively in Oak Grove (Penrose), and in patches in the Tremayne Woods and Tolvan-Wollas Wood. As in most English woods where it occurs, holly appears to be increasing, and many of the trees are putting on a foot or more of growth a year. Hollies will probably not reach the canopy: the older thickets in Calamansack are dying back. Holly is more sensitive to exposure than oak: big hollies left as standard trees by recent coppicing in Tremayne Great Wood have died back severely.

Oak–hazel wood has a thin, though often continuous, understorey

Tree community	Soil	Occurrences in England	Peterken equivalent
Pure oakwood	Very infertile	Widespread in Highland Zone	Upland birch–sessile oak woods
Oak–holly	Slightly less infertile	Widespread, chiefly in Highland Zone	Ditto
Oak–hazel	Moderately infertile	Widespread in Highland Zone	Upland hazel–sessile oak woods
Hazelwood	Weakly infertile	Widespread in Lowland Zone	Acid sessile oak–hazel–ash woods
Hazel–ash	Relatively fertile	Abundant in Lowland Zone	Acid pedunculate oak–hazel–ash woods, heavy soil form
Hazel–elm–ash	Fertile, damp	Widely scattered in Lowland Zone	Wet ash–wych-elm woods, heavy soil form (approx. equivalent)
Suckering elm	Acid, very fertile	Rare	Invasive elmwood (this category is much wider)
Valley alder	Flushed by springs	Widespread but of small extent	Base-rich springline alderwoods

Table 3 Woodland types in the Helford River woods. The third column gives the occurrence of each type of woodland in England generally: the Highland Zone comprises Cornwall, Devon, the Welsh Border, Pennines, North York Moors and Lake District. The fourth column links these woodland types to the classification of British woodland by G. F. Peterken.[105]

of hazel and occasional holly. It is typical of slightly more fertile soils, especially the upper slopes of Bonallack, Merthen and Calamansack Woods (Fig. 6.5). It is quite extensive in Tremayne Great Wood, and occurs on the near-precipitous slopes of Tolvan-Wollas Wood. We have seen that hazel has been noted, though less abundantly than oak, in Kerrier woods almost since the earliest records. Coppicing probably had the effect of encouraging hazel, which has declined since the last felling: it does not compete well with oak on these soils,[106] and does not flower in shade. Oak–hazel is a transition to the hazelwoods next to be described.

This type of woodland shows a transition to the earthworm kinds of soil that are prevalent in the remaining woods. The remaining

Fig. 6.6 Oak–holly wood in Treverry Wood, March 1987.

Fig. 6.7 Suckering elm clone in Tremayne Great Wood, September 2007.

non-oakwood types are on soils of greater fertility. Such soils, and the woodland on them, survive only as patches within oakwood.

Hazelwood, with little or no oak, was probably one of the most extensive types of Cornish wildwood. It was probably the main woodland type in Trelowarren Wood. It now occurs at the top of Merthen Wood.

Hazel–ash wood, with sallow and blackthorn, is here a woodland of damp, relatively fertile soils, especially in valleys. It is best developed on the lower slopes of Trelowarren Wood, and there are traces of its having once occurred in Trelowarren Mills Wood. It grows in the middle valley and on valley sides in Merthen Wood, and in the west of Bonallack Wood. A small patch – in which one ash-tree towers above the surrounding oaks – is on the plateau edge of Calamansack, and there is a patch similarly situated in Tremayne Great Wood.

Hazel–elm–ash wood, with elm and lime, is confined to part of Trelowarren Wood. The site is rocky and moderately acid (pH 5.1), and is irrigated by springs.

Suckering elm occupies part of Tremayne Great Wood (Figs. 6.7, 7.27). Such elms often represent the extreme in soil fertility and the herbaceous plants indicate that this is so here – though the soil is quite strongly acid (pH 4.4), it is watered by a spring. Such acid, fertile elmwood is a rare type: other examples exist on the Essex–Suffolk border.

Valley alderwood forms a ribbon along the bottom of Trelowarren Wood and the middle valley of Merthen Wood; it is absent from all the other valleys. Alderwoods are characteristic of valley bottoms, fed by springs from the sides, intermittently throughout the British Isles.

Woods throughout England have been transformed over the last hundred years by the invasion of birch. The Helford is one of the very few areas to have escaped this change. Birch is absent from many woods, and only in Grambla Wood is it moderately common. Rhododendron – that curse of many western oakwoods – is also remarkably scarce.

Alien trees
Turkey Oak was introduced to the area apparently about a hundred years ago. There has been an increase of beech and holm oak [for discussion of all these, *see* the Flora and Conservation chapters].

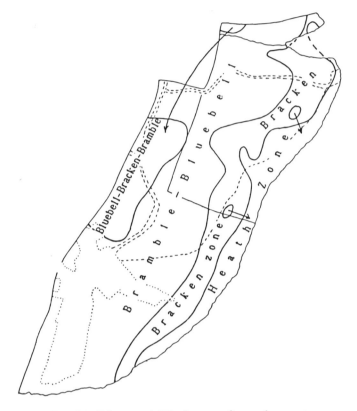

Fig. 6.8 Calamansack Wood: zones of ground vegetation.

Ground vegetation

Herbaceous plants and undershrubs form another series of plant communities. To some degree – but not closely – they are correlated with the tree communities. As with the trees, I begin with the drier and least fertile soils.

Heathy vegetation, with heather, bell heather and bilberry, forms the seaward margins of the northern woods from Gweek to Calamansack (Figs. 6.8, 6.9); this zone is broadest in Bonallack Wood. It also occurs on the lower, rocky margins of Devichoys and Cosawes Woods, proving that nearness to the sea is not the determining factor. Brambles and bluebell are absent. In places, particularly in Merthen Wood, there is cow-wheat (*Melampyrum pratense*). Usually there is some bracken, often wood spurge and even a little ivy. This plant community evidently goes

Fig. 6.9 Oak–heather in Merthen Wood East, September 2007.

with the shallowest, most infertile soils, under pure oakwood. It may depend on reduced shade from the stunted oaks.

The remainder of the oakwoods has as dominant species bracken, bramble and bluebell, and the woodrush *Luzula sylvatica*, in varying combinations and degrees of vigour. In Calamansack Wood bracken is most abundant either with bluebell on the plateau, or else with honeysuckle on the middle slopes under oak–holly. Brambles are widespread, being most vigorous under oak–hazel on the upper slopes, where ferns such as *Dryopteris pseudomas* and *D. dilatata* suggest locally greater fertility. Ivy is scattered throughout, most abundantly in the northern valley. A similar pattern is repeated in Bonallack Wood, but with rather more bluebell and ivy. Merthen, however, is a glorious bluebell wood and has rather little bramble or bracken. Woodrush (common in Welsh and Irish woods that are not grazed) is here almost limited to Tolvan-Wollas, Gweek and Tregithey Woods, where it is widely dominant, alone or with bluebell

Fig. 6.10 Dominant *Luzula sylvatica* in Tregithey Wood, September 2007.

(Fig. 6.10). Bluebell and bramble, with some bracken, are dominant on the upper slopes of the southern woods.

Ferns are particularly abundant and luxuriant. Often there is a plant community consisting of a mixture of the two male ferns, *Dryopteris filix-mas* and *D. borreri*, and their relative *D. dilatata*. Lady fern, *Athyrium filix-femina*, occurs less often as stately individuals. As befits the very Atlantic climate, royal fern, *Osmunda regalis*, grows in five of the woods.

Ash and hazel woodland, on their more acidic soils, also have bluebell and bramble. On lower slopes these suddenly give way to plants of damp calcareous woodland: primrose, dog's mercury, bugle, hogweed, enchanter's nightshade, wild garlic, strawberry, etc. (Fig. 6.11). This plant community (more characteristic of the Midlands and East Anglia) is best developed in Trelowarren Wood, and gives that wood a long species list. There are small areas of it in the valleys of Merthen Wood and a patch near the ash–hazel area in Calamansack Wood.

The elm part of Tremayne Great Wood has a suite of plants which indicate greater fertility: nettle, red campion, angelica, and unusual

Fig. 6.11 Primrose, celandine and violets in Tremayne Great Wood, April 2016 (photograph by G. F. Peterken).

vigour among brambles and ferns. Golden saxifrage grows where little springs break out.

The deep peaty soils of valley bottoms, notably in Trelowarren and Trelowarren Mills Woods, have golden saxifrage and the umbellifer *Oenanthe crocata*.

Coppicing

The following areas were coppiced between 1960 and 1990:

> *Bonallack Wood*: about 4 acres [1.62 ha] of oak cut 1962; 1 acre [0.4 ha] of hazel–ash 1976; small patch of oak 1983.
>
> *Calamansack Wood*: patch of oak in north-east corner cut *c.*1970.
>
> *Grambla Wood*: 1½ acres [0.6 ha] of oak–hazel cut *c.*1972.
>
> *Gweek Wood*: about 4 acres [1.62 ha] of oak cut 1982 or 1983.
>
> *Tremayne Great Wood*: about 1 acre [0.4 ha] of oak–hazel (with a little ash and some elm invasion) cut 1984 and 1985.
>
> *Treverry Wood*: small patches of oak felled 1986.

	Devichoys	Tremayne Gt	Gweek	Treverry
Agrostis canina	+			
Agrostis stolonifera		+		+
Betula pubescens	+++			
Blechnum spicant				+
Buddleja davidii	+			
Calluna vulgaris			+++	
Carex laevigata	+			
Carex remota				+++
Carex sylvatica				+
Chamaenerion angustifolium	+			
Cirsium palustre		(+)		
Digitalis purpurea	+	+++	+++	+++
Epilobium montanum		+		
Erica cinerea			+++	
Holcus lanatus		+		
Hyacinthoides nonscripta (Endymion)		+++		
Hypericum perfoliatum				+
Luzula pilosa	+			
Luzula sylvatica			+++	
Pteridium aquilinum			+	
Ranunculus repens		+		+
Rhododendron ponticum	+			
Rubus fruticosus	++++	+++	+++	+++
Rumex acetosella		+++		
Sarothamnus scoparius			--	
Senecio erucifolius	+			
Silene dioica (Melandrium rubrum)		+++		
Sonchus oleraceus		+		
Teucrium scorodonia	++			
Ulex europaeus	+		++	

Table 4 Coppicing-response plants in four woods. Abundance is roughly indicated ranging from ++++ (very abundant) to (+) (rare) and -- (very rare).

In each case the stools grew again, however long the interval since the previous coppicing (64 years at Tremayne, probably more at Calamansack). Regrowth was usually rather slow: oak at Gweek put on only 6 ft [1.8 m] in 4–5 years, and in Bonallack Wood reached about 18 ft [5.49 m] high and 4 in. [0.1 m] diameter in 25 years. This is to be expected with thin soils and severe exposure. However, in the sheltered Treverry Wood, oak grew up to 7 ft [2.13 m] in a year, despite having last been coppiced at least 120 years before.

Coppicing, as usual, brings out the vigour of the herbs, and awakens (from buried seed) plants lying dormant since the last coppicing. In Gweek Wood, heather, bell heather and broom appeared in an area previously dominated by woodrush. In Tremayne Wood, foxglove and sheep's sorrel came up abundantly, evidently from seed formed after the last coppicing in 1921. On this more fertile soil, brambles flourished, and were cut back by way of experiment. The long-delayed coppicing in Treverry Wood brought out foxglove and St John's wort (*Hypericum perforatum*).

In these woods, unexpectedly, heather seems not to be a coppicing plant, except for Gweek (Table 4).

Fire

Fires in England used to be common in young plantations. In natural woods they are hardly possible, for no native tree is fire-adapted. However, weak fires can occasionally happen in oakwoods if enough heather or bracken has accumulated. I have no record of woodland fires in West Cornwall, but in Calamansack Wood I found tell-tale scars on the uphill side of the bases of several oaks.

Deer

Deer are now present in most woods in England, often in unnaturally large numbers. This has had a dramatic and disastrous effect both on the regrowth of the trees and on the herbaceous plants (and even on low-nesting birds such as nightingale).

West Cornwall is very fortunate to have escaped, but will probably not remain deer-free for much longer (*see* page 143).

Fig. 6.12 Oak lignotuber in Bonallack Pill, September 2007.

Junction with the sea

West Cornwall is one of the few parts of Britain where ancient woodland meets the sea. The oakwoods usually sweep down to the low clifftop, unaltered except that service is scattered among the last oaks before the bottom. The very outermost oaks lean or hang as far as they can reach over the sea, depending on the height of the cliff and degree of wind exposure. These last oaks form massive woody bases, fantastically gnarled like a Tolkien illustration – Australians would call them lignotubers (Fig. 6.12). (Or is it that all coppiced oaks form lignotubers, but only the cliff-edge ones are exposed to view by erosion?)

The woods used to be coppiced right to the edge, though sometimes (as at Bonallack) the bottom fringe was not cut at the last coppicing. Usually there is a row of great oak stools just on the cliff's edge. This 'wall of oaks' not only terminates the woods but is prolonged outside them along the coast wherever there is a cliff – with, rarely, relict service and

Fig. 6.13 Merthen Western Pill, September 2007.

lime (*see* pages 70–2). It probably functioned as a hedge to keep beasts grazing fields or heaths from falling over the edge. Below Bonallack Wood, where the cliff is double, there are two such rows of oak stools.

In the most exposed places (e.g. on the west side of Merthen middle peninsula) the last row of oaks, stunted like those above it, roots in the clifftop and hangs down the cliff. With moderate exposure, the last, multiple-stemmed, oaks have trunks going upwards and horizontally as well as downwards. Where tall, sheltered oakwood reaches the clifftop (e.g. in Merthen Wood opposite Vellan Tremayne Creek) the last oaks arch over the sea instead of hanging down. In creeks, where the cliffs are low, the outermost oaks may grow horizontally far out over the water, or else – if they are timber trees – may topple in and remain alive for at least thirty years, resting on their boughs in the mud. Both of these are well shown in the western pill of Merthen Wood (Fig. 6.13).

These variations depend on the fact that the roots of oaks are poisoned by saltwater and have to be out of reach of the very highest tides, but the tops do not mind the occasional dip. The outermost oaks tend to grow upsidedown, with their roots higher than their tops. I have seen living boughs wetted to a few inches at high water of an ordinary spring tide. An extreme tide therefore submerges them by at least 2 ft [0.6 m] – hence the seaweeds which catch in the twigs. Holly is apparently more sensitive, the foliage being cut off at high water.

At the seaward edge various clifftop and saltmarsh plants (e.g. thrift) get into the woods. This junction is also the home of species such as wild madder, pignut and *Melittis*, whose connexion with the sea is less evident.

In Wales, Scotland and Ireland, where woods are commonly grazed, palatable plants tend to be restricted to cliffs, where livestock cannot get at them. There is no sign of this happening here.

Young trees

As might be expected, saplings are not generally abundant in these woods. Few British trees are fully shade-tolerant; new individuals arise when trees blow down or woods are felled. The Helford woods are still in a state of growing up since the last coppicing and there is not normally enough light to support seedlings of the same species as the canopy trees. The youngest trees are those established at the last coppicing. Even these may be few, because coppice stools are long-lived and turnover is slow.

Only two woods have considerable numbers of young oaks. In Calamansack, oaklings grow, often in quite large numbers, on the steep slopes just above the heather zone (Fig. 6.14). Whether they survive, even for a year, evidently depends on a nice balance of factors. At this point on the slope the canopy is thin and admits enough light for the oaklings to live but not enough for tall heather or bracken, which would overtop, shade and kill them. At present they rarely live more than three years, although given more light they would grow into trees. This has happened in the small coppiced area in this wood, which is now a thicket of pole-sized oaks.[107]

In Treverry Wood many oak seedlings have survived where felling has let in light – though not enough light to stimulate too much competition from brambles.

Fig. 6.14 Calamansack oaklings, September 2007.

In many woods in England ash flourished in the twentieth century. Ash seedlings can survive in shade for many years, even if damaged by browsing deer, waiting until the fall of a big tree allows them to get away. This is not widespread in the Helford River woods because most of the soils are not fertile enough for ash, but where it does occur young ashes are sometimes frequent. The big ash in Calamansack Wood is surrounded by a thicket of its children.

Other saplings are of trees which tolerate more shade than oak. The only locally native tree of this kind is holly, which is slowly increasing. Also increasing are non-indigenous shade-bearing trees, coming from seed shed by trees planted in or outside the woods. In Calamansack Wood, for example, beech and holm oak have arrived, evidently by nuts and acorns brought by rooks or jays from trees planted elsewhere; once germinated, they can survive under the shade of oak. Some of the beeches are now quite big trees and are starting to break through and overtop the oak canopy. Sycamore has similarly invaded parts of Tremayne Great Wood and Merthen Wood.

Fig. 6.15 Bonallack ex-Arundell wood-pasture, September 2007.

Wood-pasture

In Anglo-Saxon England wood-pasture was a frequent alternative to coppicing. As the human population rose, demand for fuel and labour available for getting it both increased, and wood-pasture was converted either into coppice-woods, farmland or heath. Surviving examples, though few, put England in the first rank of European countries for veteran trees and the special creatures that depend on them. Cornwall has only one first-class example, the ancient deer-park of Boconnoc. However, West Cornwall has enough fragments of wood-pasture to testify to their former existence.

A small area remains of Arundell Wood, the link between Bonallack and Merthen Woods (Fig. 6.15). There is a scatter of massive spreading oaks, not coppiced. Some of these are infilled with towering ashes and young sycamores. Another patch has a hazel understorey and a blackthorn thicket. Then there is a heathy patch with cow-wheat, *Veronica montana* and mosses under the oaks.

Fig. 6.16 Frenchman's Creek – secondary woodland, April 2016 (photograph by S. Leatherdale).

Although the woods around the Loe Pool are mainly obvious plantations on the Penrose estate, there are two possible remnants of wood-pasture. Oak Grove (*see* page 123) is a stand of massive oaks intermingled with big hollies: there are no coppice stools but a few may be pollards. They go down a steep rocky slope to the Loe Pool, some standing in the water when it is high. There are several huge ashes at the bottom. The flora is poor, as would be expected of a place that was first grazed and then heavily shaded as the oaks grew bigger and holly infilled. Degibna Wood, now a pine plantation over a hundred years old, has some oaks on its steep rocky base; it is on the east side of Loe Pool, centred on grid reference sw649250.

Fig. 6.17 Oak mildew (photograph by R. Griffith).

Recent woodland

Oak is a pioneer tree: it grows from seed much more easily on farmland than within existing woods. Most of the recent woodland adjacent to existing woods is oakwood. An example, of about two acres, extends Calamansack Wood to the north. In the mid-nineteenth century this was a small field lying between a row of oak stools on the clifftop and a hazel and blackthorn hedge at the back. It is now a wood of huge spreading oaks, with a thin scatter of young hazels and occasional holly and elder. (The hazels of the old hedge are among the biggest in England.) There are many such woods at various stages of development; the younger ones lack hazel. In Meneage several of them (e.g. Gearhills Wood, sw720245) have been replaced by conifer plantations.

Sallow forms recent woodland in valley bottoms that are too wet for oak. New hazelwoods occasionally appear on the more fertile soils (e.g. one of the additions to Grambla Wood). Sycamore has invaded some old fields (e.g. on Porthnavas Creek and near Tregithey Wood).

The recent woods that fill the inland valleys are a complex mosaic of oakwoods and sallow-woods, often with bracken glades and patches still unwooded. Most of them contain walls and remains of the small fields, orchards and cottages which they overlie. The great spreading oaks are often bigger than those in ancient woods, and it is easy to forget that they may be less than a century old (Fig. 6.16).

Bonython Plantation (SW699206) is typical of the more successful plantations of the mid-nineteenth century. It appears, from annual rings, to have been planted in 1856 on wet, boulder-strewn serpentine rock with small projecting tors, part of the Goonhilly Downs. The older trees are Scots Pine, *Pinus maritima* from the Mediterranean, beech, and some oak. It possibly incorporated a pre-existing grove of hazel and sallow on a patch of boulders. The wood has abundant bluebells and frequent primrose, and is rich in ferns (including royal fern) and bryophytes, but has few other woodland plants. Like most small plantations, it fell into neglect.

Tree diseases

The twentieth century brought one major change. Oak mildew (*see* Fig. 6.17), caused by the fungus *Microsphaera alphitoides,* was introduced from America in (or just before) 1908 and quickly overran Europe. This is the fungus which produces a thin whitish layer on the leaves of oaks in summer; it flourishes especially in the damp valleys. Although mildew is a relatively trivial disease, it probably makes young oaks more light-demanding than they would otherwise be.[108] To survive mildew as well as shade, they need to be under a bigger gap in the canopy than they would have done before 1908.

Elm Disease has had relatively little impact because elms are rare in woodland. The elms of Tremayne Great Wood did not escape, but are growing back vigorously from suckers.

Tree diseases are one of the two greatest threats to woodland in the future, as shown in Chapter 8.

7 Individual Woods

Bonallack Wood
19.3 acres [7.8 ha]
SW716260

The medieval farmstead of Bonallack lies in a romantic spot, at the end of steep zigzag lanes through woods grown up on what was Merthen Downs and small fields adjoining. The original wood fringes the Helford River, on steep slopes facing south and west, with moderate exposure. In the east is a ravine with a small quay; the original quay was probably in the next pill eastward (*see* Merthen Wood). The wood east from the ravine is recent but on the site of the medieval Arundell Wood.

The wood is unaltered from the 2nd edition OS map of 1811. It is shown as an ordinary wood on OS maps of 1877–8 and 1906, as well as 1973. On the 1811 OS it is shown as coppiced, unlike most other woods.

The old wood is divided into a timberwood, with huge tall oaks and ashes in the ravine, and the coppiced remainder. Part was cut in 1944, another part in 1962 and an acre in 1976; regrowth has been slow after a good start, probably because of exposure.

Bonallack is a nearly pure oakwood with not much hazel or holly. Ash is scattered in the ravine (and occasionally elsewhere), and is increasing. Rowan is occasional. There is a clone of an unusual elm at the bottom of the ravine.

Service, fringing the clifftop, is more abundant than in the other woods; it suckers and forms small clones. The lowest oaks hang down over the sea; in places the cliff is double, with a second row of oaks halfway down. There is some invasion by beech and sycamore. Beeches, as elsewhere, overtop the oaks.

The flora is rich, partly because of the junction between woodland and saltmarsh. The wood is rather brambly but with abundant bluebell; at the bottom is a narrow, well-marked heather zone.

Fig. 7.1 Bonallack (left) and Merthen Wood West, September 2007.

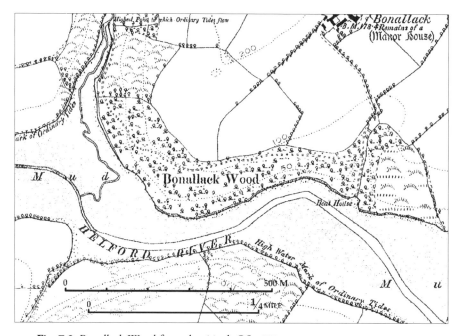

Fig. 7.2 Bonallack Wood from the 6-inch OS 1888.

The wood is documented, with no known change, back to the 1390s.[26] Its boundaries, however, are not specially massive. There are several charcoal-hearths. A sizeable quarry is accessible only by sea.

Bosahan Wood
6.828 acres [2.76 ha]
SW731297

This wood (accessible by public bridleway) occupies the west side of a valley below the Bosahan granite quarry. It is not encroached upon by the quarry. The top of the valley is filled by great mounds

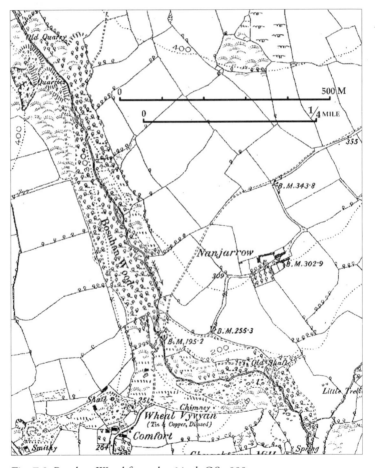

Fig. 7.3 Bosahan Wood from the 6-inch OS 1888.

of waste granite accumulated in decades of quarrying, some of them overgrown with trees.

The wood is full of industrial remains. Across the stream, in an extension to the wood, are remains of a blowing-house, with mortars (for crushing ore) and other utensils carved from granite. At the top of the wood is a constructed track (still a highway) with a leat, partly buried by quarry spoil, below it. At the south end of the wood this leat turned a gigantic overshot mill-wheel, the pit for which shows it to have been about 36 ft [10.97 m] in diameter. These are presumably the remains of the mine called Wheal Fire, abandoned and forgotten before 1878.

This is the only wood on granite. It is marked on the 1811 OS but probably does not appear on the 1649 survey of Constantine. As a wood it is disappointing and does not match its history. It is almost entirely of small beeches grown up after being once felled c. 1940, with some sycamore invasion and a very few ash and hazel stools. The flora is poor (except for masses of the moss *Hookeria*). It is a good bluebell wood. Boundary walls and banks are of little interest, except for a strong bank at the south end and two minute enclosures by the stream.

In its present state this is a plantation, but the beeches are much younger than 1811. Possibly it began as a natural secondary wood in the eighteenth century; late in the nineteenth it was made into a plantation so thoroughly and successfully that one can no longer tell what the original trees had been.

The woods of Bufton
Bufton 3.3 acres [1.34 ha] SW703286
Polglase 14.7 acres [5.95 ha] SW702285,
Tolvan-Wollas 1.81 acres [0.733 ha] SW703285

These woods line the steep slopes of one of the sheltered inland valleys that converge on Gweek and are much embedded in twentieth-century woodland. They are too small to show accurately on the 1811 OS map. The Constantine and Wendron tithe maps show that the valley bottom, now woodland, was once partly meadow. Bufton and Tolvan-Wollas Woods are in the Constantine survey of 1649; Polglase, being in Wendron, would not appear.

The woods are of oak and hazel, the hazel being mainly on the lower slopes; ash and sallow grow at the foot and have invaded the valley floor. The hazel is very well grown and polypody fern grows on it as well as on oak. Nothing seems to remain of the conifers shown in Bufton on nineteenth-century maps. Two-thirds of Polglase were felled *c.*1900.

Tolvan (West) Wood is on an exceptionally steep slope, well over 45 degrees; trees often overturn and tumble down. An even steeper ravine

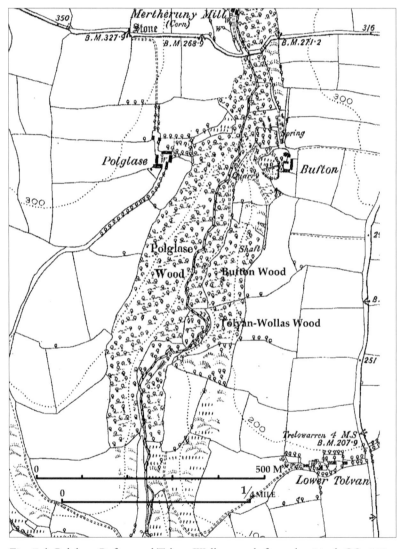

Fig. 7.4 Polglase, Bufton and Tolvan-Wollas woods from the 6-inch OS 1888.

divides it. Although tiny, it has proper woodbanks and is duly divided into a coppice south of the ravine and a timberwood to the north. It has ancient oak stools (6 ft [1.83 m]), last cut *c.*1900. The ground is covered chiefly with bluebell and woodrush, with dog's mercury in the ravine.

Calamansack Wood
32.0 acres [12.95 ha]
SW752270

A house was built in the wood in 1918. Much of the wood is mown in August on a two-year cycle. This favours bluebell at the expense of bramble. Two mowings kill holly, resulting in a characteristic empty bottom to the wood. This wood is on a steep south-east-facing slope with a plateau at the top; it is very exposed to the east, except in a deep narrow ravine down to Pill Cove. In the west are two houses of the 1930s, one of which is a period piece with its green pantile roof; their gardens have

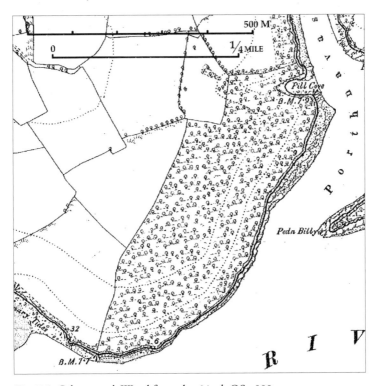

Fig. 7.5 Calamansack Wood from the 6-inch OS 1888.

Fig. 7.6 Polypody on oak, Calamansack Wood, May 2016 (photograph by S. Leatherdale).

increased at the expense of the wood. A foot-holloway zigzags down to the pill, at the mouth of which is an elegant granite boathouse.

The wood is clearly divided, and has been for at least two hundred years, into a coppice on the exposed slopes and a timberwood in the ravine. The coppice was last felled between 1820 and 1860, apart from an area *c.* 1930 and a few small patches since. The timber trees appear to date from the 1770s. The ancient stools are up to 10 ft [3.1 m] in diameter. The trees are almost all oak, with hazel and holly as an understorey on the slopes (Fig. 6.5). Service grows on the cliff edge. There is one very big ash at the edge of the plateau. Young ashes are invading the bottom of the ravine, where there ought to be a strip of ashwood as in similar ravines in other woods. There is a clone of wild cherry, one of only two in all the Helford River woods. Various non-native trees have appeared, some accidentally from nearby plantations, others planted on building the house and later. Young oaks are many but survive only where given light (*see* pages 96–7).

Fig. 7.7 Ravine in Calamansack Wood, 1986.

Fig. 7.8 View towards Calamansack Wood, middle right, July 1986.

The wood has a rich flora, including columbine and sanicle. There is a very clear zonation in the herbs and undershrubs, from bluebell on the plateau to a heathy zone near the sea. The latter has heather, bell heather, bilberry and wood sage on a black, acid, peaty soil over clay. Coppicing plants include honeysuckle and *Holcus mollis*.

Calamansack Wood is well recorded back to 1249, the longest certain documented history of any Helford River wood. With Merthen and Gweek, it is one of the earliest woods in England to be shown on a map. It has an ancient boundary bank and an internal earthwork corresponding to a sixteenth-century subdivision (*see* page 62, Fig. 4.1). There are at least three charcoal-hearths.

What did the name Calamansack mean? The 1249 form, *Kylmoncote*, makes no sense in Cornish and is evidently a misspelling. *Kylmonsek* occurs in 1308 and 1331,[109] *Kyllymansak* in 1442,[110] and in 1478 we meet a John *Kyllymonsek*.[111] The first part of the word is probably *kyl* 'corner'; *monsek* is a word of unknown meaning with the adjectival ending *-ack*. The place-name therefore means 'Something-y Corner'. By 1442 the name had been reinterpreted as if it contained *kelli*, 'grove', perhaps because of the wood. The hamlets of Calamansack Wartha and Wollas were both in existence at least by 1365[112] and finally the Kyllymonsek family was named after them.

Carminowe Wood
9.5 acres [3.85 ha]
SW665242

This may be the westernmost well-preserved ancient wood in England. The steep north-facing inland wood grows on a slaty bedrock with boulders of quartz. The boundaries are banks and walls of various dates, the south-western woodbank being exceptionally massive. At the eastern end of the wood, a deeply sunk lane is a remnant of the otherwise lost Helston–Carminowe road. The wood has probably been truncated at some time on its south side. In the middle of this side a curious embanked enclosure, now occupied by a nineteenth-century plantation, projects into the wood. On the northern side the wood has increased slightly to reach the stream at its base, which was originally excluded.

The wood is of almost pure oak (including some pedunculate oak),

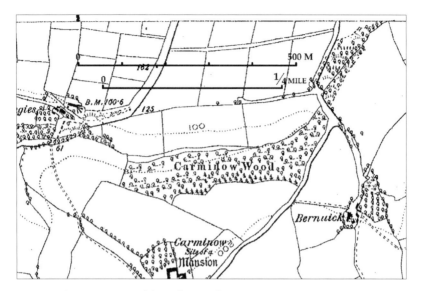

Fig. 7.9 Carminowe Wood from the 6-inch OS 1888.

with occasional holly and sparse hazel on the lower slope. Most of the stools are small and have been cut only once, in around 1910, but there are some up to 7 ft [2.13 m] across. Although inland, they are wind-pruned. There are remains of planted trees – pine, beech, sycamore – from which some beech and sycamore invasion has come. Despite the infertile soil and lack of coppicing, the flora is fairly rich, including tutsan and archangel.

All the field evidence indicates that this is an ancient wood, though it is poorly documented and was not noticed by the 1811 mapmakers.

Cosawes Wood
46.979 acres [19 ha] on OS 25 inch 1890s
SW769375
Ponsanooth, near Penryn (not a Helford River wood)

This wood had a curious use. When it was bigger than now there was a deep valley in the middle, in which the 1811 Ordnance Survey puts 'Powder Mills': doubtless making gunpowder for blasting in mines was one of the many enterprises of the Lemon family. The advantage of this situation would have been that if the mills blew up, as powder mills often did, the woodland and the valley would confine the explosion. The St Gluvias tithe map[113] of 1842 depicts 'CASAWES POWDER MILLS' in more detail, with small buildings cautiously scattered and the magazine a safe distance off in a meadow in the wood. By the 1870s the mills were disused and the part of the wood to the west had been grubbed out to make a field. There are charcoal-hearths and there is a megalithic wall in the wood's interior.

Devichoys Wood
39.5 acres [15.99 ha]
SW 772 376, near Penryn, Falmouth (not a Helford River wood)

This has been a nature reserve of Cornwall Wildlife Trust since 1988. It is on quartzite, with flushes up to two thirds the height of the wood.

As with many west Cornish woods, there is (or was) a prehistoric round on the Edgecombe Downs[114] above the wood; there are also at least three round barrows.

At some time before 1811 the Lemon family, lords of Carclew, extended the wood over the Downs by plantations of mixed conifers and broadleaved trees. The Mylor tithe map of 1842[115] depicts the plantations in detail, underlain by the hedges of former fields. Most of the extension was grubbed out between 1930 and 1958.

This wood having no ravine, the timberwood part occupies most of the bottom of the slope, except where the soils are very thin. There is hazel–ash below the leat with *Clematis*, *Arum* and *Tamus*. A great deal of *Rhododendron* has been removed. There is an oak aged 70 at around 5 ft [1.5 m] and particularly fine hollies. The charcoal-hearth is doubtful.

Grambla Wood
16.6 acres [6.72 ha]
SW693287

This is a wood of 16.6 acres [6.72 ha], plus about 30 acres [12.14 ha] of recent woodland. It is a complex of old and young woods and fields with leats. There is young oakwood (*Q. robur*). It has two charcoal-hearths with oak charcoal. Part was coppiced in around 1972.

This wood is hidden in one of the valleys behind Gweek, on a much

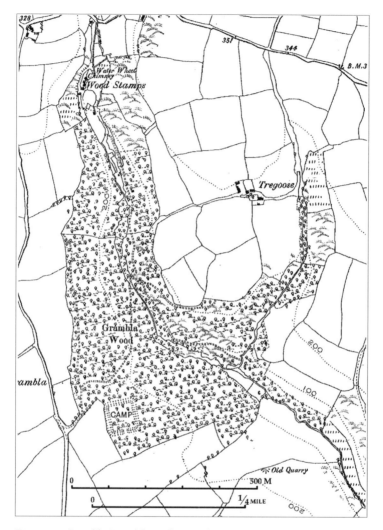

Fig. 7.10 Grambla Wood from the 6-inch OS 1888.

used public bridleway. It has a most complex history and has both lost and gained in area.

Oliver Padel tells me that the place-name Grambla is medieval; the early spelling *Gromleg'* (1327) indicates that it would be the Cornish form of the word *cromlech*, and that a cromlech once stood at Grambla farm. Grambla Wood, divided into a Great and Little Wood, is shown at slightly greater extent (at the south-west corner) than on the 1888 OS

6-inch map, covering in total 59 statutory acres [23.88 ha] at that date.[116]

According to the tithe map of Wendron, 1841, the wood occupied only the west side of the valley and extended up on to the plateau to embrace a square earthwork at the top. It was then of 44 acres [17.81 ha]. The lands on the east side of the valley, now wood, were called 'crofts': *croft* in Cornwall means an enclosure, but does not (as it does in England) imply cultivation. These crofts were described as 'furze' or in one instance as arable; one was named Woody Croft but described as furze. The narrow, flat bottom of the valley was called 'moor' and described as pasture and furze. As we shall see, this is not entirely borne out by the evidence on the ground.[117]

Much of the expansion of the wood across the valley happened between 1841 and the first edition 25 inch OS of 1876. Further fields have 'tumbled down to woodland' at various dates since then. At the same time, most of the original wood was grubbed out. The plateau portion – nearly half the original area – was destroyed between 1876 and 1920, leaving a grove around the earthwork. In the 1970s, there were further encroachments on the slope, leaving only the steepest parts as woodland.

The wood recorded in 1841 and still surviving is oak–hazel, with pure oakwood on what is left of the upper slope. Oak stools are up to 6 ft [1.83 m] across. Part was coppiced *c.*1972 and has grown well; timber trees were left among the underwood in the usual English manner. There is occasional birch and a little holly on the lower slope. One fragment, in a ravine, is of oak standard trees over holly underwood, and may represent a timberwood section. Ground vegetation is bracken, bluebell and bramble, with much ivy. Royal fern was found. At the stream the wood ends in a bank and wall, which twice crosses the stream so as to bring it partly within the wood. A very strong bank, with a ditch either side, not noticed on the 1841 map, divided the wood.[118] There are constructed tracks, and two charcoal-hearths. A cluster of shallow pits shows that somebody has been digging for minerals.

The lower part of the wood across the valley is, in part, definite oak coppice with stools up to 5 ft [1.5 m] in diameter, last cut in 1930 and *c.*1900; there is a little hazel. It is an excellent bluebell wood and the only part of the wood where I have seen wood anemone. In this portion are two constructed tracks and a charcoal-hearth. The schedule to the 1841 map calls this area Croft and describes it as 'furze'. However, the

Fig. 7.11 Grambla Wood looking south-east across the wood, March 1987.

wood cannot have reached this state of development and of use in 150 years. This is one of two places in these woods where the documents are at variance with the field evidence. It looks as if the tithe map surveyors ran two pieces of land together.[119]

The remaining parts of the wood have mostly grown up, to various states of development, since they were described as 'furze', 'pasture' and 'arable' in 1841. Some areas are of oak, as timber trees only, with no sign of coppicing. The bottom of Woody Croft is long-established hazelwood, which could have given its name to the field in 1841. Other former fields have grown up to hazel, sometimes sparse among bracken. The valley bottom, former 'moor', is oakwood with no sign of coppicing; the ground, with several stream-courses, is uneven, as though dug over for stream tin. Unlike other woods, this has no ash along the stream.

Gweek Wood
50.6 acres [20.48 ha]
SW705259

Gweek Wood stands at the head of the Helford River, next to the port of Gweek (some of whose buildings have encroached on the wood). Most of it has been coniferised; the rest is almost pure oakwood, with some holly and ash, and a little alder in a side-ravine. There was an earlier attempt at replanting, of which a few big firs survive.

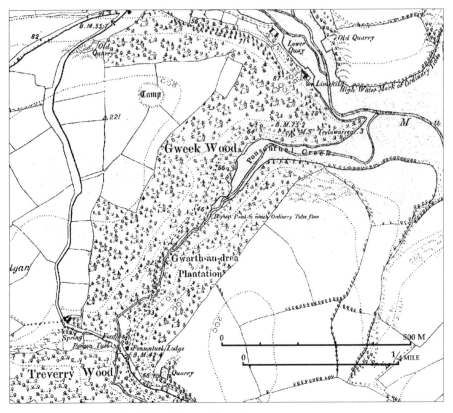

Fig. 7.12 Gweek Wood from the 6-inch OS 1888.

Gweek Wood is shown on the Falmouth map of *c*.1545. On the Mawgan tithe map of 1838 it appears as 'Coppice Wood'. It had then recently been bisected by Gweek Drive, now a public main road.

The surviving wood is largely oak coppice, last cut in around 1940. There is an area without oak stools, but whether this is ancient timberwood or any stools went with the replanting cannot now be told. The wood varies in exposure, the eastern point being extremely exposed with fully grown oaks no higher than a man.

Gweek belongs to the northern group of woods, with very acid soils and heathy vegetation. Heather, bilberry and bell heather abound, except where there are tracts of woodrush (*Luzula sylvatica*).

About four acres were coppiced in the early 1980s – the best recent example of coppicing the heathy type of wood. Oak regrowth was surprisingly good, considering the exposure. The heath plants flourished.

Fig. 7.13 Gweek Wood sea edge, September 2007.

Fig. 7.14 Bluebell and anemone under beech in Gweek Wood, April 2016 (photograph by G. F. Peterken).

Fig. 7.15 Merthen Middle Pill, September 2007.

Merthen Wood
(East and West) 143.6 acres [58.11 ha]
SW730261

Merthen is the largest and most impressive of the woods, fringing the Helford River for 1½ miles [2.41 km]. The wood faces generally south, but with the various ridges and ravines there is a great variety of aspect and exposure, with the west half less acidic. It is private and little visited, but much of it can be seen from a boat.

There are three pills at the foot of ravines, with constructed tracks leading down to them. The main river access was the deep hollow lane through East Wood to the quay at Merthen Hole on the main Helford River. There are two buildings at Groyne Point and a track to them. A ridgeway was visible at Groyne Point in 1980.

The wood is very largely of oak, mainly coppiced, with giant stools up to 14 ft [4.27 m] across. The last major coppicing was in the 1930s, but

Fig. 7.16 Merthen Woods West, East and North from the 6-inch OS 1888.

some areas have not been cut since the 1820s. The oaks exhibit the widest variety of stature (Fig. 6.2c). Holly forms a sometimes dense understorey on parts of the lower slopes, and hazel on the upper slopes; at the top of the wood are areas of hazel without oak. There are occasional rowans and alder buckthorn is locally frequent. North of Middle Pill in West Wood there is a giant stool of smallish-leaved elm on a boundary.

The ravines follow a pattern. Each has a timberwood area – the tallest oaks in the wood – on its upper and middle slopes. Then comes a zone of tall ashes, sometimes with hazel. The middle ravine has a lowermost zone of alder. There are a very few elms in the ravines and a small clone of Cornish Elm at Merthen Quay.

Beech and sycamore have been invading the wood for about a century, with the beech rather less invasive than the sycamore; they probably began in a small area of the mid-north, where conifers on the 1877 map indicate some planting. Some of the beeches are starting to tower above the oaks. Ash also tends to increase, but young oaks are few.

This wood has all the possible variants of oak meeting the sea – most romantically in the western pill, with great trees growing horizontally or layers of fallen oaks successively toppled into the mud. Service and alder buckthorn are scattered among the last row of oaks at the cliff edge.

This wood is the richest on the Helford River in flowering plants and ferns. Some of the rarities have been mentioned (*see* page 74). Other species include bitter vetch *Lathyrus montanus*, betony *Stachys betonica*, royal fern *Osmunda regalis* and the sedge *Carex pilulifera*. Hay-scented buckler fern *Dryopteris aemula** is locally abundant. *Luzula sylvatica* is exceedingly rare here. Mosses and liverworts, though luxuriant, are apparently less notable, but include a good quantity of *Hookeria* in the lush ravines.

Leptura orulenta (longhorn beetle) and *Serrion ferrugineum* have been reported by Keith Alexander (Exeter). Also recorded is *Anchonidium unguiculare*, a weevil, unique in the British Isles.[103] There is also *Andrena praecox,* a bee that specialises in *Dipsacaceae*. *Nomada ferruginata* is a parasite on it (Red Data Book). *Limax cinereoniger*, a slug said to be an indicator of ancient woodland, is reported from Groyne Point.

This is a marvellous bluebell wood, especially under hazel. Brambles

---

* [Oliver Rackham indicated some uncertainty about the species identification here.]

and bracken occur in places and there is a seaward fringe of heather and bilberry, less well developed than in Bonallack Wood. The ravines are zoned, with dog's mercury and nettle on the sides and *Oenanthe crocata* in the peaty mud at the bottom; golden saxifrage is abundant in flushes.

Merthen Wood, in Cornish *Coesenys, Coose-Carminowe* and *Cosabnack*,[120] is well documented back to the fourteenth century. It has probably changed little in area, although the boundary banks and walls are of various types. East and West Woods are divided by a wall alongside the middle stream; various other internal walls and banks probably indicate divisions of ownership which had been re-amalgamated by the sixteenth century. The three Cornish wood-names are likely to refer to these divisions. At an early date Carminowe manor somehow got hold of one of these sections of the wood: the 1570 court case clearly shows that its wood was juxta Merthen and was not the present Carminowe Wood.[121]

The quay and buildings at Merthen Hole would well repay further study. I have not yet found the charcoal-hearths which Henderson saw.

The wood ends westwards in a great bank, evidently the boundary with Arundell Wood. A deep holloway crosses the bank and goes off towards Bonallack. On the bank, mysteriously, are several stools of wych-elm, a rarity in Cornwall. Most of the woodland beyond the bank is less than a century old, but a few gigantic hazel stools may be relics of Arundell Wood.

Merthen Wood
(North) 24.4 acres [9.87 ha]
SW733269

This wood is very different from the rest of Merthen Wood. It consists of timber trees of oak, very widely spaced and spreading, with a thin understorey of hazel and locally holly. There is no sign of any coppicing except for the fringe of oak stools above the sea. At the top of the slope the wood thins out into bracken glades. Here are gigantic spreading beeches, among the most magnificent in Cornwall, with limbs arching high overhead and then taking root; they are beginning to decay and display the beech fungi *Oudemansiella mucida* and *Ganoderma*

Fig. 7.17 Oak woodland, Merthen Wood West, September 2007.

adspersum. There are also a few big pines. The strip of woodland connecting this with the East Wood is of similar oaks, invaded by sycamore.

The whole wood is very sheltered. The pill at the bottom is little visited, with great oaks leaning far out over the water and layers of oaks in the mud. This creek seems not to have been used for a quay.

The uphill side of the wood has a bank and ditch, probably an outwork of the ancient earthworks one field away.

This is a secondary wood. It is not on the OS of 1811 nor in earlier surveys, but on the Constantine tithe map (1842) it appears as 'Northern Wood'. The beeches and pines must have been planted, very soon after 1811. The wood seems to have arisen by natural succession (oak, hazel, holly) combined with a partly successful plantation. It would have been a source from which beech and sycamore have invaded other woods. It has not been managed for many years; the abundant fallen trees and great rotting logs make it an excellent habitat.

Oak Grove, Penrose
12.3 acres [4.98 ha]
SW649259

This can be seen on the way to Penrose (National Trust). It is the only wood on the Penrose estate which has some claim to be ancient woodland. It slopes down to the delta of the River Cober, where the north end of the lake has silted up in recent centuries. It is of short, massive oaks, interspersed with great hollies, many of which have recently been felled by the National Trust. The flora is very poor. There is no coppice structure, but some of the oaks may be pollards.

The documentary evidence is inconclusive. There was a Penrose Wood and a Penventon Wood somewhere in the area in the thirteenth century.[122] The eighteenth-century 'Helston Lake' map[123] shows what is undoubtedly this wood but as a thick scatter of trees rather than actual woodland. I suspect that this is an old secondary wood that grew out of a field containing pollard oaks.

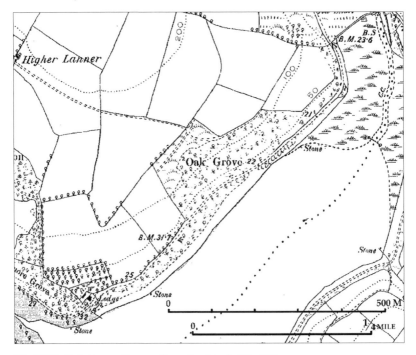

Fig. 7.18 Oak Grove, Penrose from the 6-inch OS 1888.

Polglase Wood, *see* **Bufton Wood**

Polwheveral Wood
9.5 acres [3.84 ha]
SW736285

A beautiful little wood hidden in a steep remote valley. It appears in the 1649 survey of Constantine. There are three charcoal-hearths. The wood used to be of 11.7 acres [4.73 ha] and adjoined the small wood of Polwartha (Table 2), but in recent years the Polwartha part has been lost to agriculture and a corner of the remainder to a sewage-works.

It is a well-preserved, if rather sparse, coppice of oak and oak–hazel,

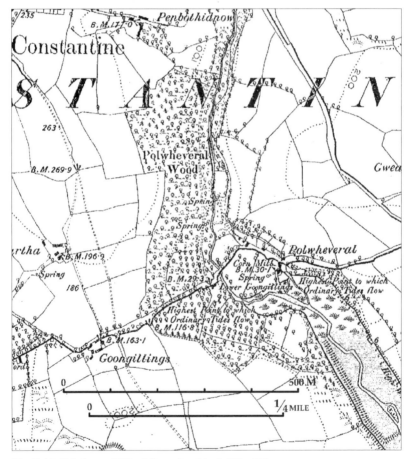

Fig. 7.19 Polwheveral Wood from the 6-inch OS 1888.

with sparse hazel and ash. Oak stools (including some pedunculate oak) reach 6 ft [1.8 m] in diameter. It was last coppiced around 1920. There is some sycamore and Turkey Oak. Bluebell, bramble and ferns are abundant.

Roskymmer Wood (alias Reskymmer Wood)
38.6 acres [15.62 ha]
SW698248

This inland wood faces south-east, descending a steep slope to a meadow, now overgrown. It is conspicuous from roads and footpaths on three sides. At its north side it slopes north-east into the bottom of a minor valley, ending at a lane. It was last coppiced in around 1930. In the 1960s, the wood was coniferised. In two-thirds of it there was partial success: most of the planted trees lived (including *Abies*, oak and beech), but many

Fig. 7.20 Roskymmer alder valley, September 2007.

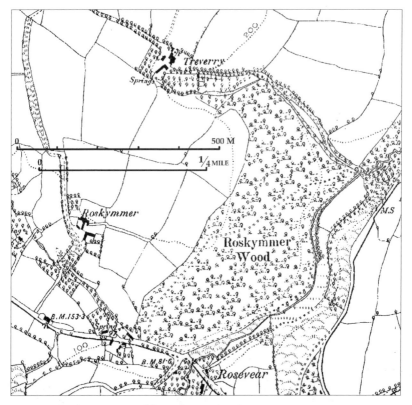

Fig. 7.21 Roskymmer Wood from the 6-inch OS 1888.

existing trees withstood poisoning. The remainder, in which planted trees (if any) came to naught, is partly intact coppice-wood, partly relics of an earlier attempt at replanting. There had been an earlier planting of beech. Timber trees had probably been scattered among underwood in the English manner.

The surviving wood is predominantly oak–hazel, with some holly and a little rowan. On the plateau is one of the best examples of old hazelwood on the Helford. The bottoms of the slopes have alder fringes. The north end of the wood is invaded by sycamore, with Lizard and Dutch elms suckering from the lane. Ground vegetation is predominantly bluebell and bramble, but this is the only inland wood to have a heath zone on the lower slope. The bottom of the northern valley is swampy. At its junctions with the former meadow and the lane the wood has massive woodbanks.

Tolvan-Wartha Wood
5.3 acres [2.15 ha]
SW710283

The valley below Tucoyse is full of small fields in various stages of growing up to woodland, of elm groves and habitation sites, of waterworks and at least one ruined mill. Embedded in this is a small ancient wood, one of the woods of Tolvan-Wartha. The 1842 tithe survey of Constantine lists four woods here; the other three (including the curiously elongated 'Tolvin Coppice Wood') are now fields. Some of these were probably 'The Woods', of less area, belonging to Tolvan-Wartha in the 1649 survey. The woods may have been too small to appear on the 1811 OS. On the 1887 OS map it is shown as 'rough grass'.

The wood is steep, with sandy soil. It is an oakwood, with sparse coppice stools and many young standard trees dating from the last

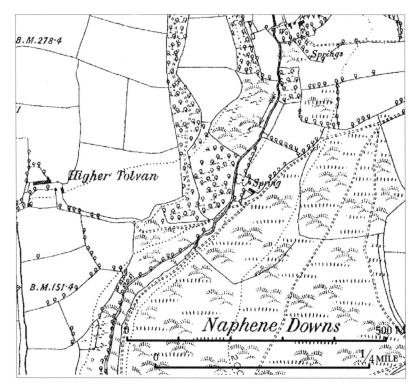

Fig. 7.22 Tolvan-Wartha Wood from the 6-inch OS 1888.

coppicing *c*.1860. The ground is less strongly acid than usual, with abundant dog's mercury. There are woodbanks all around except on the north-west. The wood is crossed by a constructed track from a clapper bridge at the bottom. There is quite a rich flora, including royal fern.

The adjoining wood to the south is almost identical and has big oak stools up to 6 ft [1.8 m] across. It is no less an ancient wood and I can only suppose that the schedule to the tithe map listed it as a field in error for one of the other groves. (There were about three thousand numbered fields and woods in Constantine, and it would have been easy to transpose two of them.)

The other surrounding woods are of oak and sallow and are post-1842; this includes the bottomless sallow swamp below the wood.

Tolvan-Wollas Wood, *see* Bufton Wood

Tregithey Wood
6.0 acres [2.43 ha]
SW778251

This National Trust wood is reached from the west by walking along the side of Gillan Creek, through a most instructive series of small fields in various stages of growing-up to woodland.

The north-west-facing wood slopes steeply down to a 'wall' of big stools at the top of the cliff, whose trunks grow out horizontally over the sea. It is of almost pure oak with a little hazel and holly. Coppice stools are rather sparse, not cut for at least a century. The east end of the wood lacks stools and was evidently the timberwood; it is not in a ravine, but the whole wood is relatively sheltered. Small though this wood is, and difficult of access, it has a constructed track through the middle and at least one charcoal-hearth.

The flora appears to be poor. The whole wood is carpeted by the giant woodrush *Luzula sylvatica* to a greater extent than any other on the Helford (Fig. 6.10).

The east end of the wood adjoined a round, now (with part of the wood itself) built over by the suburbs of Gillan.

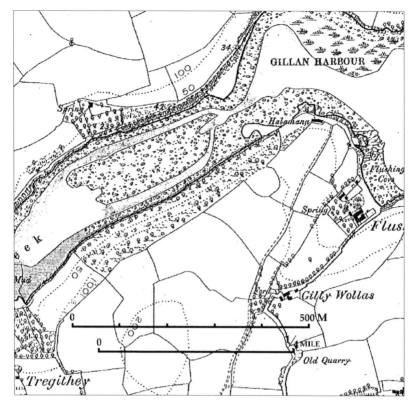

Fig. 7.23 Tregithey Wood from the 6-inch OS 1888.

Trelowarren Wood

20.7 acres [8.38 ha]
SW724241

This wood lies in the valley below Trelowarren House and runs into side-valleys. It covers only the south-west side; the other side, below Caervallack round, is not ancient woodland and is now coniferised. Trelowarren Wood was one of the most remarkable ancient woods of the Helford River, the only one with a rich flora of calcicole plants. Much of it, alas, was replanted in the 1950s, and because it was the home wood of a planting family its story is confused by trees introduced at earlier times, although not throughout the wood.

There is now remarkably little oak. Oak, if it was dominant, would have occupied the upper slopes, now coniferised. Most of the surviving

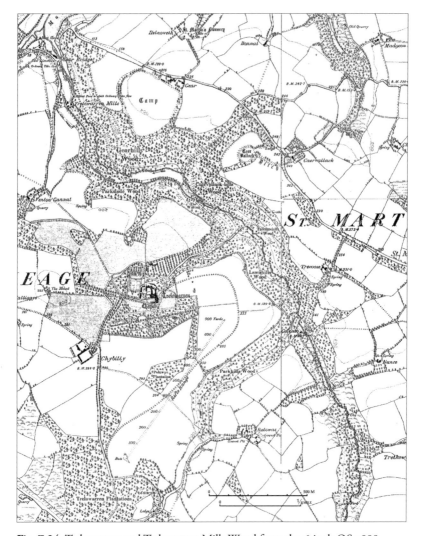

Fig. 7.24 Trelowarren and Trelowarren Mills Wood from the 6-inch OS 1888.

native woodland is of hazel and sallow on the lower slopes, with alder along the stream. It was coppiced in 1956. The hazel zone is rich in native trees, including the only lime and wych-elm in these woods. Ash is rapidly increasing. Some of the earlier plantations are of interest, for example the great curiosity of a cherry-laurel coppice.

The wood has a very rich flora (*see* page 72). Ground vegetation is varied, with bluebells on the upper (replanted) slope, and elsewhere

Fig. 7.25 Trelowarren Woods, September 2007.

patches of ramsons, wood sorrel, dog's mercury, and golden saxifrage in flushes. There is also orpine and solomon's seal.

The wood ends up-slope in a bank with a great ditch, which has long served as a boundary to Trelowarren Park. This ditch could be the outwork to an otherwise unknown Iron Age round under or near Trelowarren House. The wood has various other earthworks and internal walls, and was evidently subdivided.

At its south end, the wood turns into giant oaks with little underwood. This area has a complex history, with a profusion of walls. Conifers on the 1878 OS map show that there has been planting. This part is heavily grazed and has little ground vegetation except at the bottom, where a patch of ramsons still marks the Pool of the Wild-Garlic recorded in the charter of AD 977.[124]

Trelowarren Mills Wood
25.1 acres [10.16 ha]
SW720243

Hidden in the valley below Gear, the father of hillforts, is this steep narrow east-facing wood. It covers one side of the valley, extending into side-ravines; the opposite flank, Gear Hills Wood, is a plantation (now replanted) on the site of the heathy Gear Hills, which extended up to the outworks of Gear. The wood descends almost to the stream;

through it runs a disused leat to the watermills at the lower end, which were still grinding corn in 1906.

The trees are great oaks (both species), ashes and firs, and immense beeches. There is a thin understorey of hazel but very little coppice structure. Many giant trees have fallen and have opened gaps in which young ashes and sycamores flourish.

This wood is less strongly acidic than most. Dog's mercury is abundant in the ground vegetation, with ramsons at the bottom. Ferns are prominent. Springs break out on the slopes, with flushes of deep, soft peat full of golden saxifrage and *Oenanthe crocata*. The wood is specially noted for its wealth of mosses, liverworts and lichens, which flourish on the damp trunks and rotten logs.

The wood has a complex history and not all of it is ancient. Many of the trees date from an early nineteenth-century planting. Even in 1838 the tithe surveyors could not decide whether it was a wood or a plantation.

When I last visited the wood, in 1972, it was magnificent and distinctive as a result of a replanting, which at first succeeded, but then was neglected for over a century.

Tremayne Great Wood
10.2 acres [4.13 ha]
SW730257

This is a National Trust wood. It faces north on a steep, rather sheltered slope down to the sea, just reaching the plateau at the top.

The trees are mostly coppice, last cut in 1921, now grown up some 75 ft [22.86 m] high on the lower slopes. There are no distinct timber trees. The wood is principally of oak or oak–hazel on the upper slopes and hazel–ash on the lower; there is a large clone of a peculiar elm (*see* page 70 and Fig. 7.27) near the bottom, and some invasion by Lizard Elm at the top. This is a fine bluebell wood, with abundant bramble and ivy. There is no heath zone, despite the acid soils. The elm area is marked by nettle, elder and ferns, with vigorous bracken. The flora is not particularly rich, perhaps because fertile soils allow strong-growing species to become excessively dominant.

Coppicing was resumed in 1984 and 1985 in oak–hazel on the plateau. The growth of all species was remarkably good, especially after

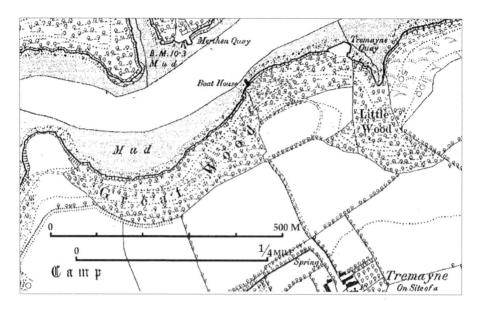

Fig. 7.26 Tremayne Great and Little Woods from the 6-inch OS 1888.

the long lapse of time; oak reached over 5 ft [1.5 m] high in two years. The coppicing flora was strong, especially in plants such as red campion, foxglove and furze, which come from buried seed.

The wood does not have particularly strong boundary earthworks, except on part of the inland side, where there is the outwork of a round. There are two great beeches on the eastern woodbank. A constructed track runs through the middle of the wood.

The way to this wood leads through the 'Vallum' Tremayne valley, with woods of magnificent youngish oaks, from which sycamores and conifers have recently been felled. These woods are mostly of the 1830s and 1840s.

Tremayne Little Wood
5.8 acres [2.35 ha]
SW735258

This wood is also accessible to the public. It was originally separate from Great Wood but is now joined by a grove of nineteenth-century beeches, in which there is a clone of elm like that in Great Wood.

Little Wood lies in a small side-valley of the Helford; a holloway

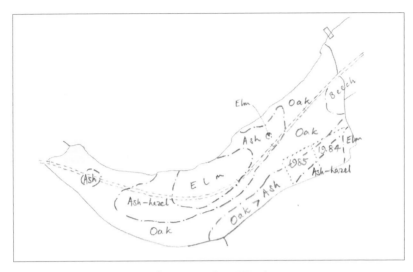

Fig. 7.27 Tree communities of Tremayne Great Wood.

Fig. 7.28 Tremayne Woods from Merthen Quay, September 2007.

zigzags down on the east side to the creek at the bottom, the predecessor of the nineteenth-century Tremayne Quay on the main Helford River. The strong boundary walls and earthworks of the wood incorporate part of the outwork mentioned above. The wood was replanted early in the nineteenth century, mainly with beech. There are some remains of the previous coppice-wood: ash–hazel, with oak stools on the upper slopes. The wood has a poor flora. It is, however, a good bluebell wood, with magnificent ferns (*Dryopteris pseudomas*) and deep swampy hollows full of *Oenanthe crocata*. Although, being a small wood, it is not on the 1811 OS, enough is preserved to establish it as an ancient wood.

Treverry Wood
25.6 acres [10.36 ha]
SW703253

This is a steep wood on one side of a valley, embedded in recent woodland. It is mainly oakwood, with alders and ashes where a spring breaks out on the slope. The oakwood is of the hazel and holly variants,

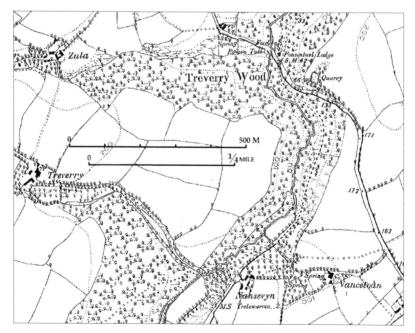

Fig. 7.29 Treverry Wood from the 6-inch OS 1888.

and is relatively fertile, with plants such as dog's mercury and barren strawberry. Oak stools are rather thinly spaced, last cut at various dates between 1860 and 1910. This is one of the most sheltered of the woods, and the oaks have grown fast, reaching 80 ft [24.38 m] in the bottom of the valley. They are mantled in lichens, mosses and polypody.

Although poorly documented, this is undoubtedly an ancient coppice-wood. It has big oak stools and is surrounded by ancient banks and walls.

Recently, some small patches have been felled; this has produced some of the most striking coppice regrowth and coppicing plants (*see* page 93), the more remarkable for the long interval since last coppicing.

This wood, with its surrounding, now full-grown recent oakwoods, is familiar to everyone who has been to the Lizard; the modern road southwards from Gweek to Coverack passes through it (sw7025).[125] The ford at the bottom completes a scene of Arcadian beauty such as even West Cornwall rarely surpasses, marred only by the unsightly widening of the track across the middle of the wood.

Under Wood
5.9 acres [2.39 ha], excluding recent woodland
SW756257 south-west of Helford

This is an east-facing wood on one side of a sheltered valley; the north end runs into a steep, boggy ravine watered by springs. The bottom of the valley is a recent hazel–ash wood; the opposite side is an old plantation of big beeches and chestnuts. Public footpaths pass the wood.

Under Wood is of oak mixed with invasive beech and sycamore, occasional ash and chestnut, and some big hollies. It is not a coppice, except that most of the beeches and sycamores were felled *c.*1930 and have grown again. The wood is bounded by walls and banks like the 'hedges' of fields. A track runs up through the wood past a small quarry or mine.

The flora is poor except in ferns, but this is the only Helford wood except Calamansack to contain wild cherry.

Although documented to the early nineteenth century, this wood has not the characteristics of ancient woodland and is probably not much older. It is a beautiful bluebell wood and the many big fallen trees make it a good habitat.[126]

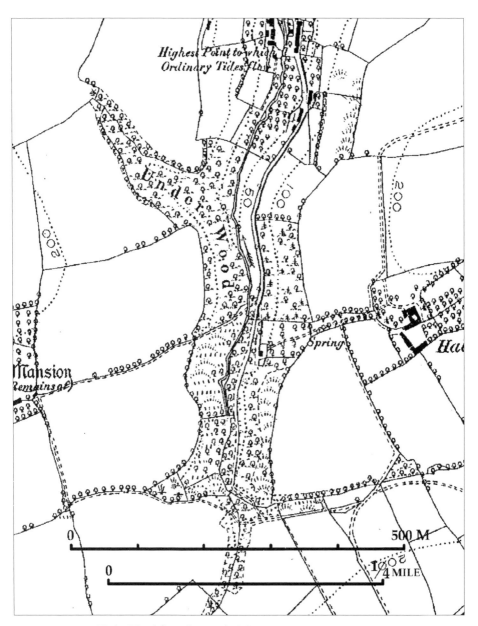

Fig. 7.30 Under Wood from the 6-inch OS 1888.

8 Conservation

The value of the Helford River woods

The Helford River woods are part of one of the most famous and most loved of English coastal landscapes. The unbroken canopy of the oaks and the great trees at the water's edge delight residents and visitors alike (Fig. 8.1, 8.4). No less beautiful are the glorious bluebells and other wild flowers, and all the variety of terrain and structure within the woods. The hidden woods in the valleys, although fewer people find them, are equally part of the beauty and mystery of Cornwall.

Some of the woods, such as Gweek and the Tremayne Woods, are much visited by the public; others are very private. Merthen East Wood must be one of the least-visited big woods in England. But these northern woods are no less of a public amenity, for every part of them is visible from the river or overlooked from some public place on the south side. And for their external appearance the recent woods are as important as the ancient woods.

The scientific importance of these woods lies chiefly in there being a large area of native woodland beside the sea. Coastal ancient woods are remarkably uncommon in England, or indeed anywhere in western Europe. (In the Norwegian fjords, which are sheltered and much less tidal, the junction between woodland and the sea is very different.) These woods have a great variety of soils, structures, plant communities and effects of wind and spray. They are intact, and have escaped almost all the grazing (which has ravaged most of the western oakwoods of Britain and Ireland) and the worst of the replanting. Besides the already mentioned rare plants and the weevil *Anchonidium unguiculare* (found nowhere else in the British Isles), the Helford woods have two beetles and two snails associated with ancient woodland. Several other rare invertebrates have been found in Merthen Wood.[103]

The hand of modern forestry has been heavy on the woods of Cornwall. According to the Nature Conservancy Council's inventory, 52 per cent of

Fig. 8.1 Merthen Wood across the Helford River, April 2016 (photograph by G. F. Peterken).

the area of ancient woodland in the county has been lost to replanting since 1930.[127] This includes almost all the large woods; surviving woods are small and usually isolated. Only two big areas of woodland have escaped coniferisation: the Helford River woods and those of the Fal estuary and its branches. Oakwoods often have little resistance to replanting and most of the coniferisation of Cornwall has apparently succeeded. In contrast, the native trees of the Helford woods have usually resisted replanting with some success (e.g. Reskymmer Wood).

The three most important individual woods are Merthen Wood, Tremayne Great Wood and Trelowarren Wood. Merthen is the only one at present scheduled by the Nature Conservancy Council as a Site of Special Scientific Interest; it is also a Grade 2 site in the national Nature Conservation Review. But it would be wrong to conclude that some woods deserve a higher standard of conservation than others. The long list of special features in Merthen partly depends on its having been more fully investigated. As with their qualities in the landscape, the woods form a group, and damage to one of them would diminish their value as a whole. In logic, there should be a Helford River Site of Special Scientific Interest comprising all the ancient woods adjoining the river.

The woods are also an antiquity; they are a record of Cornish history from its beginnings. This applies not only to the artefacts (woodbanks, charcoal-hearths, mill remains, etc); the coppice stools and vegetation also preserve an archaeological record. Woods are not a random collection of trees which were put there in some arbitrary way, but are full of meaning, much of which remains to be discovered.

The conservation of woods of this kind implies maintaining their historic character, both against deliberate destruction and against such natural changes as are inconsistent with that character. To some extent the present structure of the woods is not intrinsic to their character but is a temporary consequence of their being of so many years' growth since last felling, which is bound to change as the trees go on growing. The proportions of holly and ash will also change and can be allowed to do so (within limits) without encroaching on the historic character. But to destroy the oak stools and to substitute a spruce plantation or an oak plantation would not be consistent with the conservation of the woods; nor would allowing the woods to turn into beechwoods or birchwoods through doing nothing.

In thus defining the *genius loci* of the Helford River woods, I do not despise other kinds of Cornish landscape such as Trelowarren. Trelowarren is one of the most exquisite of landscape parks, but its beauty is of the formal kind which comes from deliberate design and tree-planting in the last two hundred years on a previously open site. Cathedral beeches and towering conifers and brilliant rhododendrons belong to the *genius loci* of such a park. The Helford River is not a park; it is a relic of an older and wilder Cornwall, in which beech and *Pinus radiata* have no place. Both types of landscape should be properly understood; they present quite different conservation problems, and the differences between them should be upheld.

Threats

As I have shown, the apparently timeless character of the Helford River landscape is somewhat of an illusion. The woods have been less intensively used in the last hundred years than at any time in the previous thousand years. However, over a timescale of decades, the stability is real: photographs taken in 1980 are almost identical to the present state (even at the level of individual trees) despite two of the severest storms on record in the interval. It would be difficult to make out that the woods are in any immediate danger.

In 2008 I published a review of threats to ancient woodlands around the world. These came under ten headings, all of which except for two (depletion; fire and lack of fire) have some relevance to West Cornwall. The eight others are as follows.

Deliberate destruction

The risk of destruction by development has receded. Tremayne Woods belong to the National Trust, Merthen Wood is a Site of Special Scientific Interest and Calamansack Wood has a Tree Preservation Order. Development elsewhere would hardly get planning permission. Destruction by agriculture, although it has occurred (Grambla Wood), was never much of a risk in this terrain and (as in England as a whole) the risk has greatly receded.

The chief threat for two hundred years has been destruction by modern forestry, which has largely disappeared. Times have changed since 1948 (*see* page 21): most of what was then embarked upon as 'economic forestry' has turned out not to be economic; and economics themselves are no longer so naïvely accepted as a short-cut to decision-making. The Forestry Commission itself not only supports the conservation of surviving ancient woods, but since 2005 has, as a matter of official policy, supported the rehabilitation of ancient woods that it had earlier replanted.

Cornwall is full of forestry schemes which were begun and then abandoned as circumstances changed and enthusiasms waned. Most landowners would now be deterred (as they often were not then) by the practical difficulties in this terrain of destroying the existing trees and preventing them from growing again, planting new trees, keeping them alive, and finally getting the timber out. Replanting solves no long-term problems; as Trelowarren Mills Wood shows, woods that have had trees planted into them become more difficult to maintain than those that have not. Any threat of replanting in the sensitive coastal woods results in immediate and vehement public protest. See, for instance, the correspondence about Calamansack Wood in *The Times*, January 1981. These coastal woods have never grown much timber; even in Cornwall there are many easier and quieter places to make plantations.

Pollution and eutrophication

These take various forms. Past industries farted out sulphur dioxide, copper and arsenic dust, and many other noxious chemicals, especially in East Cornwall and to some extent in the West. How far these permanently affected the woods is difficult to say. The industries are extinct, but some of the heavy metals may still be there.

As in most places, woodland water tables are probably polluted by seepages of farmyard and cesspit effluent, which over the centuries are likely to have brought phosphate and contributed to the nettle beds in many ravines. More recently, fertiliser dust blowing from fields may be responsible for the cleavers and (less often) ground ivy which now grow in many woods.

At present, West Cornwall, with its prevailing winds off the Atlantic, should have among the cleanest atmospheres in Europe, as witness the profusion of bryophytes and lichens that occur on the Lizard, many of them sensitive to sulphur or acid rain. My impression is that the woods are not as rich in lichens as they might be. In north-west Europe as a whole, ammonia pollution from large numbers of livestock is apparently

Fig. 8.2 The lichen *Teloschistes flavicans* (image: public domain from Wikipedia).

a recent phenomenon, although here it ought to be long-established. The dense canopy of the oakwoods would discourage some pollution-sensitive species such as *Lobaria pulmonaria*, which are light-demanding and grow best on free-standing trees. Paul Gainey [a local naturalist] reports the magnificent and very pollution-sensitive *Teloschistes flavicans* near Merthen Wood (Fig. 8.2).

Excessive shade

This has two aspects: (i) the general lack of felling, and consequent lack of opportunity for coppicing plants to renew themselves; and (ii) overgrowing of permanent glades and open areas.

Whether the West Cornwall woods had a well-developed coppicing flora is unclear. Some plants, such as heather, cow-wheat, the two figworts, and several *Hypericum* species, which elsewhere come up from buried seed, here seem to be permanently present. *Euphorbia amygdaloides*, a common member of this category, seems not to be recorded in these woods, although *E. hyberna* does occur here in one of its very few sites in Britain. Recent re-coppicings often result in only brambles (*see* page 93).

Plants of permanent open areas have fared very badly. The 'elfin' woodland fringes, with dwarfed oaks on thin soils, however, have a number of them, including betony and saw-wort.

Deer

Deer are closing in on West Cornwall. Occasional roe-deer are reported from Devichoys Wood, where holly and other coppice regrowth has been browsed, and from Bonallack. Red deer have been for some time at Trelowarren, and one has been reported in Merthen. Muntjac – now probably the most widespread deer in England – are likely to appear soon.

In Mesolithic times, of course, two species of deer would have been present: nobody knows in what numbers. But for well over a thousand years deer have been confined to places like Merthen Park, and woodland ecosystems have become adapted to living without them. It might be said that a few deer would restore an element of naturalness that is missing from the medieval and modern landscape. However, experience (both in Britain and from Texas to Japan) shows that it is exceedingly difficult to have only a few deer. The modern countryside, with its mixture of woods and fields, is excessively favourable to deer, and, if there are any, they cannot be prevented from multiplying. There are now vastly more deer in England than in the Middle Ages. They shelter in woods, eating up the palatable plants and tree shoots and saplings, and when these are gone they go out into the fields and eat their fill of grass and crops. It would be very unfortunate if the only deer-free part of England were to be the Isle of Wight.

Invasive species

Whether by design (as with rabbit and grey squirrel in England) or by accident (mice and rats), *Homo sapiens* tends to mix up all the world's biodiversity. Often they do not merely 'enrich' the native fauna and flora but get out of hand and displace native species. Relatively few introductions from other countries become invasive, though, once they do, attempts to exterminate them are very rarely successful and even control imposes an indefinite burden on future human generations. Sometimes they hybridise with native plants to create new and even more invasive species. Compared to other countries, England has been let off lightly, but Cornwall rather less lightly than the rest of the country.

Almost every wood contains sycamore (from Central Europe) and beech (either from Europe or from the rest of England). Both perform rather better than oak and are slowly taking over the woods. Although sycamore is mainly confined to fertile ravines, the beech takeover seems to be unstoppable because oak has lost its ability to grow from seed within existing woods (*see* page 101). Beech and sycamore are significant habitats in themselves, yet it is hard to imagine that they will replicate either the ecological or the spiritual distinctiveness of the Cornish oakwoods.

Rhododendron is a much more immediate threat. It has become one of the most severe invaders of woodland in Britain and Ireland. It is extremely difficult to get rid of: cutting it down is useless, it resists weedkillers, and is forever spreading through its tiny, very fertile seeds. Only after felling and several poisonings does it finally give up. Fortunately, the only one of these woods much affected is Devichoys, where volunteers of Cornwall Wildlife Trust have put in endless hours, with some success, in killing it.

Turkey Oak has been introduced from various parts of the Mediterranean, beginning (it is said) in 1735. Its main significance is as the alternate host of gall-insects that damage native oaks (*see* page 148).

Among herbaceous plants, I have mentioned elsewhere the threat from variegated archangel, already better established in West Cornwall woods than the native plant. There is a similar threat from *Endymion (Hyacinthoides) hispanica,* the Iberian lookalike of bluebell (which it used to be bad manners to grow in one's garden), which gets thrown out and displaces, or hybridises with, the 'real' bluebell. Iberian bluebell is present in the area, but I cannot say how far it has got into woodland.

Calamansack Wood has had a house and garden in it for most of the twentieth century and so inevitably has been exposed to exotic plants and newly created species more than the other woods. *Hydrangea macrophylla,* originally a cultivated freak from a rare Japanese endemic plant, and *montbretia,* an artificial hybrid between two species of *Tritonia* from South Africa, have been replacing the native shrubs and herbs.

Infilling of savanna

The conversion of wood-pasture to forest is a widespread phenomenon from Texas to Australia: it is a matter of concern because it results in the loss of species that require both trees and open ground, and also because the existing ancient trees get overshadowed and killed by young trees arising around them. West Cornwall has a tiny example (Arundell Wood).

Climate change

If Cornwall has followed the rest of Britain, temperatures have risen by about 1.5 °C in the last hundred years. What does this mean? What would happen if temperatures were to rise, as seems likely, by another 1.5 °C?

In its simplest form, let us imagine that every day next year is 1.5 °C warmer than the same day this year. This would be barely noticeable by people (though readily measurable). What would be its ecological effects? Most of Cornwall's woodland trees and plants are well away from their southern climatic limit and would not be at risk from a warmer climate catching up on them.

However, there has been a change in phenology – in the time of year at which things happen – which is likely to continue. Oaks used to come into leaf well into May, but now do so in April. Leaf-fall changes, which are partly triggered by shorter day length, have been smaller and more variable. In Cornwall, with its warm winters, many plants now go on growing all through the winter.

It is sometimes said that changes in phenology will upset the balanced timing of the annual cycles of the creatures that make up ecosystems. I am not persuaded that there is such a balance. Stability in climate should not be assumed to be normal. Plants and animals have lived through greater differences both in climate, such as the various phases of the Little Ice Age, and in weather (the difference between one year's weather and the next). The future, however, will exceed this range in that hot years are expected to be more frequent, and cold years less frequent, than at any time since the last Ice Age.

Cornwall, especially the far south-west, already has a tendency for rainfall to be at a minimum in summer. Compared to the Mediterranean, summer rainfall is still substantial, but increasing seasonality might lead to droughts happening every summer. (This actually happened earlier in the Holocene in Spain and Greece.) This would probably not lead to radical changes in the woods: deciduous oakwoods are common in Mediterranean climates. It might, however, reverse the tendency for holly and beech to increase, while working in favour of the increase in holm oak and Turkey Oak.

Globalisation of plant diseases and pests
Readers will know the oak mildew that spreads like a thin coat of whitewash over the leaves of oaks in late summer (Fig. 6.17). This is the visible form of a microscopic fungus, *Microsphaera alphitoides*. A little over a hundred years ago this was known only to those few mycologists familiar with American tree diseases. It crossed the Atlantic in about 1908, suddenly spread all across Europe, and has never looked back. It was at about this time that oak appears to have lost its ability to reproduce within existing woods. Oaklings appear easily enough everywhere except in woodland: in fields, heaths and, embarrassingly, along railways (giving rise to special slow-running 'Leaf-Fall Timetables' in autumn). But in most woods, an oak less than a hundred years old is now a rarity. What was it that changed around 1900? I conjecture that the reason is that mildew, although seemingly a trivial disease, is death to seedlings already contending with shade: a shaded oakling without mildew lives, but with shade and mildew together it dies.

Human interference in biodiversity, including tree diseases, has unforeseen and disastrous results. Loss of oak regeneration has not in a hundred years visibly altered the Cornish oakwoods, nor will it in another hundred years; but oaks are probably not immortal, and the logical outcome will be their replacement by beech and sycamore – also introductions – and holly.

In the 2000s, the fashionable threat was from *Phytophthora* species. *Phytophthora* is a genus of water-moulds, microscopic fungi that attack plants in various ways and sometimes on a gigantic and tragic scale. The leaf-destroying *Ph. infestans* came from America in 1845, ravaged the potato crop (itself of American origin), and caused the Irish potato famine. One of the great ecological tragedies of the twentieth century was the introduction of *Ph. cinnamomi*, a common tropical pathogen, to the unique and amazing ecosystems of south-west Australia, which had no resistance to it.

There can be no doubt of the seriousness of alder disease, caused by *Ph. alni*, which was eating up alders along English rivers in much the manner of Elm Disease. How far it has got in Cornwall I do not know. It illustrates a peculiarly sinister feature of *Phytophthora*, that when species are brought together from different continents they hybridise and create a new and unknown species that may be more virulent than its parents. In this way, the harmless native *Phytophthoras* may be given teeth that they did not have.

The famous *Phytophthora ramorum* has been spreading through California, where it is called Sudden Oak Death, although it is more characteristic of rhododendrons, besides affecting many other species. Its origin is unknown; it seems not to be native to California and it, too, may be a species newly created around 1980. It has got into various European countries including Cornwall, where it affects mainly rhododendrons. A rhododendron-killer might be no bad thing, but it seems not to kill the rhododendrons (nothing does!) and spreads from them to other hosts. It rarely, if ever, affects native trees. In sojourning here it seems to have created Cornwall's own new species, *Ph. kernoviae*, also mainly on rhododendrons.

Oaks may not be much at risk from the new *Phytophthoras* (although one does sometimes find near-dead oaks with the characteristic tarry or dried-blood exudate of attack by some other *Phytophthora*). However, in my student days there was much talk of Oak Wilt, caused by the

Fig. 8.3 Knopper galls on oak (image: public domain from Wikipedia).

fungus *Ceratocystis fagacearum*, related to Dutch Elm Disease. It was devastating oaks in America, behaving as an introduced disease, although its origin was unknown: what would happen if it got here? We thought it would probably not do too much damage, since it kills chiefly American red oaks and live oaks, rather than the white oaks that are related to European oaks. Fifty years on, this is still the position: parts of the eastern States and Texas are missing their oaks, nobody knows where it came from, and it has still not crossed the Atlantic.

The introduction of Turkey Oak may have a more lasting consequence than merely a few more exotic oak trees: it brought with it the Knopper-gall insect, *Andricus quercuscalicis*. In its classic state this creature spends one year on Turkey Oak and then flies off to lay its eggs in the infant acorns of a native oak: these acorns turn into galls, which the Germans call Knopper from their likeness to the rugged acorn-cups of the Mediterranean oak *Quercus macrolepis* (Fig. 8.3). Knopper galls, however, seem now to occur on oaks well away from Turkey Oak, suggesting that the insect has now acquired the ability to do without its introduced host. It thus repeats the story of the marble-gall insect, *Andricus kollari*, which also lives on oaks. Marble galls were imported by the shipload for centuries from the east Mediterranean to make ink, but the insect did not get established until the nineteenth century, apparently because it needed Turkey Oak to complete its life cycle. It is now common everywhere, whether there are Turkey Oaks or not. Marble galls do not affect the acorn and are harmless, but Knopper galls damage the production of viable acorns by native oaks, which adds yet another burden to their already inadequate reproductive system.

Scores of such stories could be told all over the world. There can be little doubt that the spread of pathogens is, in the long term, the most widespread of all threats to the world's trees, both wild and planted. It suddenly and randomly subtracts species after species from ecosystems. As has been truly said, 'Introductions are forever': it is almost unknown for any exotic tree disease to be exterminated or even controlled once established. [For ash dieback *see* page 172, note 129.]

Natural changes
Are the woods destroying themselves or falling to pieces through neglect? I have searched for evidence that they are, and can find none – taking into account how woods work and how they got into their present state. There are no gaps or dying trees. There are frequent dead stems and occasional dead stools but most of these have been dead for many years; they are the result of crowded trees competing with each other, in or around the fifth decade after coppicing, and some of them losing the struggle for space. Growth is slow and many oaks exhibit the 'bunched-foliage' symptoms of trees that are struggling with adversity, but both of these are amply explained by exposure to salt gales. Honey-fungus is present, as it is in every ancient wood, though does no visible damage.

The scarcity of saplings is in no way abnormal, for in most English woods young trees are not present all the time. These woods, in general, are already fully stocked and there is no room for more trees.

The woods have existed for many centuries, and are robust; we can discount any risk that they will disappear through neglect and turn into something not woodland. Neglect causes woods to increase. But there is the possibility that the woods may change their character in more subtle ways. Is it reasonable to expect them to remain oakwoods for ever?

For several decades, birch and holly have been increasing in existing woods, especially oakwoods, all over England. In West Cornwall there is very little birch. Holly is increasing, but it is an ancient inhabitant of these woods and some degree of increase is perhaps to be welcomed. As noted at Calamansack, holly may well limit itself before it encroaches on the historic character of the woods.

What, then, will happen to these woods if nothing is done? No rapid changes can be expected: trees grow slowly in West Cornwall and one has to look carefully to tell whether a wood was last coppiced in the 1820s or the 1920s. What happens in the long run cannot be predicted with certainty, because no woods in Britain have remained unmanaged for much longer than some of these. An informed guess is that nothing much will change until at least the twenty-second century. There will then come a time when the oaks will start to die or (more likely) will rot and be broken by storms. It is in the nature of oak that individual stems will die or break here and there, rather than whole areas at once. This will give an opportunity for young oaks (and possibly other native trees) to arise in gaps. The result will be a wood more varied in age than at present, but still recognisable as a Helford River oakwood.

Could an exceptional storm, like that of 16 October 1987 in south-east England, blow down whole areas at once? It is difficult to draw a comparison: the blowdowns in the 1987 storm were either in oak *plantations*, with a different root structure from natural oakwood, or in woods of other species. Mr Nigel Davies [a local resident] tells me that a great storm blew down areas of oak at Watersmeet, Lynmouth, Devon in the late 1970s, but the long-term consequences are not known. We do not know whether blowdowns are possible in the woods of West Cornwall, which ordinarily, every two or three years withstand gales comparable to the 1987 storm in Surrey. The lessons to be learnt from this storm are: (i) natural woodland is less at risk than plantations; (ii) old oaks, if anything, are less vulnerable than middle-aged or young; (iii) most uprooted trees survive, and often flourish in their new orientation; (iv) oaks tend to save themselves by shedding boughs, and promptly sprout to repair the loss; (v) more damage was done in woodland by well-meant tidying-up operations than by the storm itself. I predict that if a blowdown were ever to happen on the Helford River, the woods would recover within a few years and would not lose their beauty or meaning. Management should not be specially adapted to countering this possibility.

Effect of plantations on native woods
Plantations, even if they do not replace native woods, can act as a source of shade-bearing exotic trees – beech, sycamore, rhododendron, holm oak – which get into native woods and take them over. Beech has already begun to invade, and is taller and more wind-resistant than oak. It is likely slowly to replace the oaks. This process is not compatible with the conservation of the Helford River oakwoods. The beechwood which would be the ultimate result is well represented in other parts of England, is not specially Cornish, and lacks the character and meaning of the ancient oakwoods.

Retreat of agriculture
A threat to the Helford River landscape, though not directly to the woods, comes from the depression in agriculture, which has already begun and is likely to continue. This is not to be welcomed as it might be in prairie-farming regions. This part of Cornwall is a stronghold of traditional small-scale farming of a kind now rare in England. The local farmers have, on the whole, lived in sympathy with the antiquities, natural features and wildlife which still exist in abundance on their land. Farmland and hedges are as essential a part of the Helford River scene as the woodland.

The Helford River farms have survived previous depressions with, at most, some retreat of cultivation from the most difficult soils. An objective of conservation should be to see that nothing worse happens this time. If this fails, and whole farms disappear, the temptation should be resisted to use the land for modern forestry. As I have already remarked, plantations of conifers or other exotic trees would be altogether out of place on the Helford River; they would also be too small and too remote to assure economic success. (Foresters have already laboured in this area for two centuries, and have had little, commercially, to show for it.) Any plantations should be of oak so as to give the illusion of continuing the existing woods. Better still would be to do nothing, which (as abundantly proved in the past) would create natural oakwoods at no cost.

A better solution still might be to use the land for rough pasture, with only just enough livestock to prevent trees from invading. In this way there is some hope that the now almost-vanished heaths of the Helford River commons might return.

Conservation and management

Coppicing

Should coppicing be resumed? It is how the woods have come to their present state, and is probably the only way to maintain the unbroken oak canopy into the distant future. It rejuvenates both the trees and the ground vegetation, and encourages many flowers, birds and insects, which flourish in particular stages of regrowth.

Recent experiments have shown that coppicing works perfectly well here; it could in practice be resumed throughout the old oakwoods except for the timberwoods. A great advantage is the absence of deer. The Helford woods exactly bear out the Forestry Commission's conclusions from experiments around Dartmoor and Exmoor:

> In general, the age of a stump appears not to influence coppicing potential. The most important considerations are to provide full protection from browsing and for there to be adequate overhead light. If oak trees have been coppiced in the past, resumption of this practice is quite feasible even after a hundred years of neglect.[128]

But the case for coppicing is not as strong as in other parts of England. Herbaceous plants flourish already in the uncoppiced woods, probably because the warm winters allow them to do much of their growing while the trees are still leafless. Coppicing, especially in the ravines, would be detrimental to the lichens, mosses and liverworts which are a speciality of Cornwall – many of these require long-undisturbed trunks of larger diameter than coppice stems. In this terrain coppicing would often be difficult to arrange in practice, would be highly visible, and would almost certainly be unpopular in many places. I therefore hesitate to propose re-coppicing as a general treatment.

The National Trust has begun coppicing the plateau part of Tremayne Great Wood, one of the few parts of the ancient woods that cannot easily be seen from outside. The work has been carefully and stylishly done, with thinning of the young shoots and cutting back the brambles. This experiment should be encouraged, and perhaps extended to other woods, to find out how far more general coppicing would be feasible and beneficial.

From the National Trust's experience it appears that an area of at least

Fig. 8.4 Looking south along Polwheveral Creek with Merthen Wood in the distance, October 2008 (photograph by P. Tompsett).

half an acre should be cut at once to get the full effects of coppicing. For a combination of reasons – historical, the nature of the ground vegetation, the oak mildew problem, exposure to windblow, the bryophyte and lichen habitats – the case for re-coppicing is strongest in areas of moderate exposure. Sites should be discreetly selected to avoid making obtrusively visible gaps in the canopy. The ravines should be left undisturbed for long periods as they have been in the past.

Discouraging exotic trees, including beech

Shade-bearing exotic trees are a long-term threat. No further introductions should be made, and self-sown introductions should be eliminated as opportunity offers. The National Trust is now considering the replacement of the old beech plantation between the Tremayne Woods (which will fall to pieces in the next few decades and is not self-sustaining) with oaks which will give the impression of native woodland. Likewise the big *radiata* pines, which are so intrusive on the skyline of Tremayne, should not be replaced when their time comes.

Doing nothing

The woods survived from 1920 to 1980 because they belonged to private owners, most of whom were content to leave them alone. So far this has succeeded in conserving the woods. Although not quite the ideal policy for the long term, doing nothing has much to be said for it. Those owners who still wish to leave their woods alone should not be reproached nor urged to do something 'positive'.

Neglect has the great advantage of producing rotten trees and big fallen logs, which are most important habitats for animals and plants. These can be abundant in old plantations (Trelowarren Mills and Merthen North Woods). A plantation can turn into an excellent place for wildlife, provided that after early success it falls into neglect. It becomes a good habitat by failing in its commercial purpose as a plantation; this happens by accident and cannot be legislated for. While we should do our best for the future of the Helford River woods, let us not forget that these, like all woods, have a life of their own independently of our schemes.

Annotated Maps

The thick line on each of the following maps marks the limit of ancient woodland.

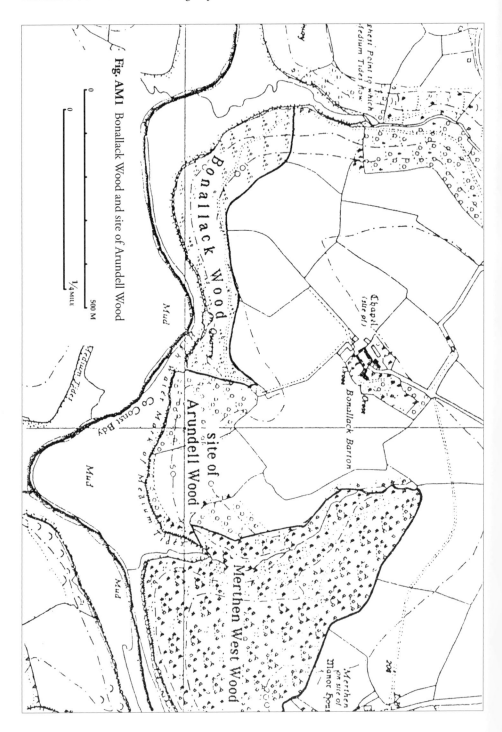

Fig. AM1 Bonallack Wood and site of Arundell Wood

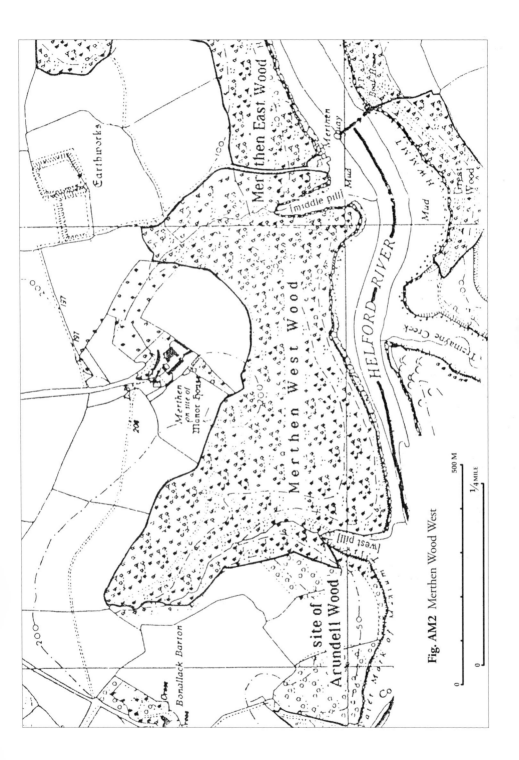

Fig. AM2 Merthen Wood West

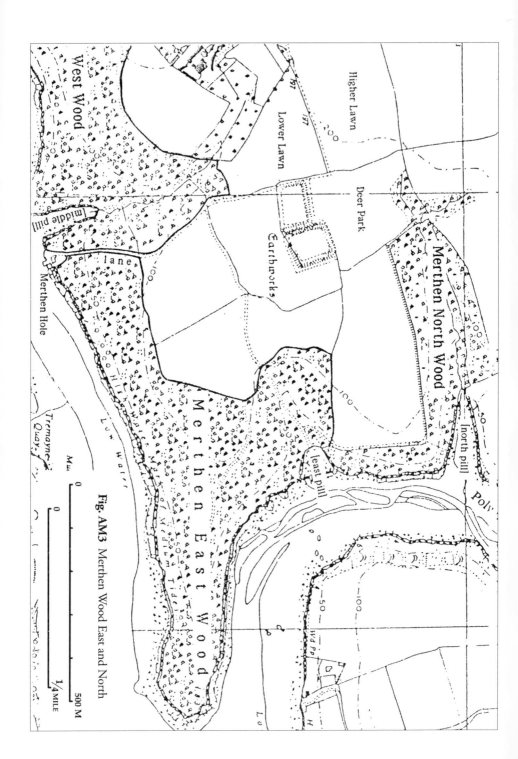

Fig. AM3 Merthen Wood East and North

West Wood

Higher Lawn

Lower Lawn

Deer Park

Earthworks

Merthen North Wood

middle pill

lane

Merthen Hole

[north pill]

[east pill]

Poly

Merthen East Wood

Tremayne Quay

0   500 M

0   ¼ MILE

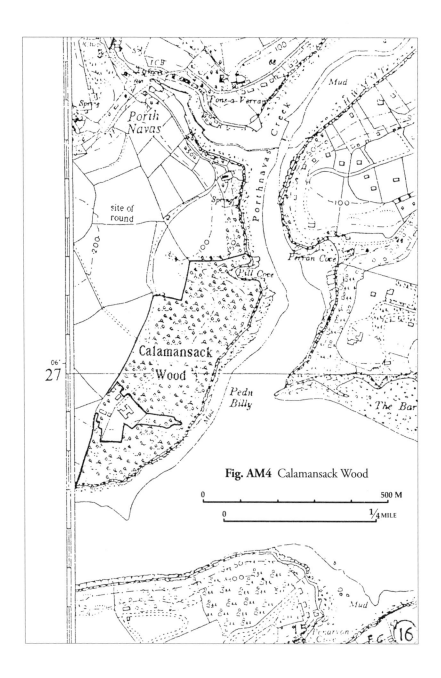

Fig. AM4 Calamansack Wood

0   500 M

0   ¼ MILE

Fig. AM5 Tremayne Great and Little Woods

Bibliography, notes and references

BIBLIOGRAPHY

Coppins, S. and Coppins, B. J. (2012) *Atlantic Hazel: Scotland's special woodlands*, Atlantic Hazel Action Group, Kilmartin.

du Maurier, D. (1941) *Frenchman's Creek*, Gollancz, London.

Henderson, C. (1935) 'An Historical Survey of Cornish Woodlands' and 'Cornish Deer Parks', pp. 134–51 and 157–62 *Essays in Cornish History* eds. Rowse, A. L. and Henderson, M. I., Clarendon Press, Oxford.

Henderson C. (1937) *A History of the Parish of Constantine in Cornwall*, Royal Institution of Cornwall, Truro.

Holden, P., Herring, P. and Padel, O. J. (2010) *The Lanhydrock Atlas*, Cornwall Editions, Fowey.

Peterken, G. F. (1981) *Woodland Conservation and Management*, Chapman and Hall, London.

Rackham, O. (1975) *Hayley Wood: its history and ecology*, Cambridge and Isle of Ely Naturalists' Trust, Cambridge.

Rackham, O. (1976) *Trees and Woodland in the British Landscape*, Dent, London.

Rackham, O. (1980) *Ancient Woodland: its history, vegetation and uses in England*, Edward Arnold, London.

Rackham, O. (1986)a *The History of the Countryside*, Dent, London.

Rackham, O. (1986)b *The Woods of South-East Essex (The Ancient Woodland of England)*, Rochford District Council, Rochford.

Rackham, O. (1989) *The Last Forest: the story of Hatfield Forest*, Dent, London.

Rackham, O. (1990, revised edition) *Trees and Woodland in the British Landscape*, Dent, London.

Rackham, O. (1998) 'Savanna in Europe', *The Ecological History of European Forests* (ed. Kirby, K. J. and Watkins C.) pp. 1–24, CAB International, Wallingford.

Rackham, O. (2003, 2nd edition) *Ancient Woodland: its history, vegetation and uses in England*, Castlepoint Press, Colvend.

Rackham, O. (2006) *Woodlands* (New Naturalist 100), Collins, Glasgow.

Steven, H. M. and Carlisle, A. (1959) *The Native Pinewoods of Scotland*, Oliver and Boyd, Edinburgh.

Tubbs, C. R. (1968) *The New Forest: an ecological history*, David and Charles, Newton Abbot.

NOTES AND REFERENCES

All notes and references by Oliver Rackham, unless noted with **Ed.**

CAD: *Catalogue of Ancient Deeds*

CoRO: Cornwall Record Office, Truro

ECH: Henderson, C. *Essays in Cornish History* (1935) edited by Rowse, A. L. and Henderson, M. I., Clarendon Press, Oxford.

RIC: Royal Institution of Cornwall, Truro

1 Henderson, C. (1935)a 'An historical survey of Cornish woodlands', *ECH* pp. 134–51.

2 Dunham, K. C. and Gray, D. A. (eds. 1972) 'A discussion of problems associated with the subsidence of south-eastern England' *Philosophical Transactions of the Royal Society of London* A272 pp. 79–274.

3 Coombe, D. E., Frost, L. C., Le Bas, M. and Watters, W. (1956) 'The nature and origin of the soils over the Cornish serpentine' *Journal of Ecology* 44(2) pp. 605–15.

4 Unpublished report by G. F. Peterken on Calamansack Wood, July 1980.

5 Staines, S. J. (1984) *Soils in Cornwall III*: sheets sw61, 62, 71 and 72 (The Lizard) Soil Survey Record 79, Harpenden.

6 Rackham (1986)a pp. 68–71.

7 French, C. N. (1985) *Cornish Biological Records: The sub-fossil flora of Cornwall and the Isles of Scilly*, Institute of Cornish Studies.

8 Rackham (1998).

9 Vera, F. (2000) *Grazing Ecology and Forest History*, CAB International, Wallingford.

10 Mitchell, F. J. G. (2005) 'How open were European primeval forests?' *Journal of Ecology* 93 pp. 168–177.

11 Oliver Padel says: about the statements 'the many elm-groves on the Lizard and elsewhere', and earlier 'Part of the same slope … is elmwood …': "would it be desirable to check whether these present-tense references to elm and elmwoods are still true today or do the observations date perhaps from Oliver Rackham's earlier visits? I know that some damaged elm can regrow (there are some around us here in St Neot), but (as far as I know, sadly) it does not now form 'elm-groves' in anything resembling their earlier form. But it may be that these statements were deliberately and knowingly made." This may be research worth pursuing. **Ed.**

12 Hogg, A. H. A. (1975) *Hill-Forts of Britain*, Hart-Davis, London.

13 Saunders, C. (1972) 'The excavations at Grambla, Wendron 1972: interim report' *Cornish Archaeology* 11 pp. 50–2.

14 For charters in general *see* Rackham (1986)a p. 309.

15 Oliver Padel also suggests reference to: Finberg, H. P. R. (1963, 2nd edition) *The Early Charters of Devon and Cornwall*, Leicester University Press, Leicester; and Hooke, D. (1994) *Pre-Conquest Charter-Bounds of Devon and Cornwall*, The Boydell Press, Woodbridge. **Ed.**

16 Oliver Padel says: "The later of these two references (above, ref. 15) is currently the standard work for anyone to use, since it gives full texts and complete references to earlier editions and discussions; but I do not know whether Oliver Rackham actually used it or merely relied on the nineteenth-century editions that he refers to." **Ed.**

17 Davidson, J. B. (1883) 'On some Anglo-Saxon charters at Exeter' *Journal of the British Archaeological Association* 39 pp. 259–303.

18 Simon Leatherdale says he finds this comment surprising: in 2016 he found wild garlic to be common in woods in the Helford River area – but perhaps Oliver's comment is that it is not common in ancient woodland, only recent secondary woods in the area, where it does indeed seem to be common. **Ed.**

19 For details *see* Rackham (1986)a pp. 310–3.

20 Henderson (1937) pp. 157–8.

21 Oliver Padel's information.

22 *CAD* A.10405.

23 Henderson (1935)a (op. cit., ref. 1).

24 The spot was near the junction of the A3083 and B3291 roads.

25 Rowe, J. H. (ed., 1914) *Cornwall Feet of Fines*, Vol. 1, editor's translation, Devon and Cornwall Record Society. (I am grateful to Mr O. Padel for drawing my attention to this document.)

26 Oliver Rackham originally said that the wood of Benadlek is attested to in 1386; Oliver Padel says that this is, in fact, a reference to the barton of Bonallack, not the wood, which is mentioned later in the 1390s in the undated deed, *Catalogue of Ancient Deeds*, IV, no. A.10409. A recently erected 'park in the land of Bannellec' (presumably a deer-park) is also mentioned rather earlier, in 1303, and Oliver Padel expects that Oliver Rackham would have wished to mention this here, had he known of it. (Same *Catalogue of Ancient Deeds*, IV, no. A.10282.) (Bonallack, the habitation, is mentioned in 1386–7 but only as a licence being granted to the lord for a chapel at his house there; for some reason Oliver Rackham seems to have fastened onto that reference as being to the wood, which is not mentioned in the source of that date.) **Ed.**

27 *CAD* A.10409. Editor's summary.

28 Henderson (1937).

29 Henderson (1935)a (op. cit., ref. 1).

30 Rackham (1980, 2003).

31 Hull, P. L. (ed., 1962) *The Cartulary of St Michael's Mount*, Devon and Cornwall Record Society, Mounts Bay.

32 CoRO: Ddrp/7 p. 86. (With thanks to O. Padel.)

33 Ric: Henderson MS HE/3/2. (Ditto.)

34 Barton, D. B. (1971) *Essays in Cornish Mining History*, D. Bradford Barton, Truro.

35 Henderson (1935)a (op. cit., ref. 1).

36 Not the same as the present plantations and woods of Clowance park.

37 Information from Veronica Chesher.

38 Original is British Library MS Cotton Aug. 1 i 38; published in Rowse, A. L. (1969, 2nd edition) *Tudor Cornwall*, p. 399, Macmillan, London.

39 Leland, J. C. (1545) *Itinerary* [republished 1907, Smith, L. T. (ed.), London].

40 There is a Polpeor Cove at Lizard-Town.

41 Oliver Rackham originally said here: "The deer-park was somewhat of a rarity in Cornwall, which, like other poorly wooded regions, had had very few medieval parks" and refers to Leonard Cantor's book on deer-parks, Cantor, L. (1983) *The Medieval Parks of England: a gazetteer*, Department of Education, Loughborough University of Technology, which does list very few deer-parks for Cornwall. However, Oliver Padel doesn't think it is true that there were very few medieval deer-parks in Cornwall. He says that Henderson maps some 57, but plenty more are known. **Ed.**

42 Cantor, L. (1983) (op. cit., ref. 41).

43 Henderson, J. (1935)b 'Cornish Deer Parks' *ECH* pp. 157–62.

44 RIC: HF/16/42.

45 The places are identified with the help of the Tithe Survey. Mr J. C. Lyall tells me that there are still fields called Deer Park, Higher Lawn and Lower Lawn.

46 RIC: HF/16/7.

47 CoRO: TT/4.

48 CoRO: TT/4.

49 Davidson (1883) (op. cit., ref. 17).

50 RIC: HF/16/34 [a copy of the original, made *c.*1700].

51 Rackham (1986)a p. xv.

52 Penhallurick, R. D. (1986) *Tin in Antiquity: its mining and trade throughout the ancient world with particular reference to Cornwall*, The Institute of Metals, London.

53 Carew, R. (1602) *The Survey of Cornwall*, S. S. for John Jaggard, London.

54 Barton (1971) (op. cit., ref. 34).

55 Hopkins, J. J. (1980) 'Turf huts in the Lizard district: an alternative suggestion for their interpretation' *Journal of the Royal Institution of Cornwall* 8 pp. 247–9.

56 Lewis, G. R. (1908) *The Stannaries: a study of the medieval tin miners of Cornwall and Devon*, University of Cambridge.

57 Hatcher, J. (1970) *Rural Economy and Society in the Duchy of Cornwall 1300–1500*, Cambridge University Press.

58 Todd, A. C. and Laws, P. (1972) *Industrial Archaeology of Cornwall*, David and Charles, Newton Abbot.

59 Barton (1971) (op. cit., ref. 34).

60 Rogers, J. E. T. (ed., 1882) *A History of Agriculture and Prices in England, from the Year After the Oxford Parliament (1259) to the Commencement of the Continental War (1793)*, Vols. i-vii, Clarendon Press, Oxford.

61 Brown, E. H. and Hopkins, S. V. (1956) 'Seven centuries of the prices of consumables, compared with builders' wage-rates' *Economica* 23 pp. 296–313.

62 Lewis, G. R. (1908) (op. cit., ref. 56).

63 Oliver Rackham originally said 'the centre of tin production moved westwards from Dartmoor to Land's End' – Oliver Padel says 'this is broadly true but "Land's End" is too precise; there was plenty of tin production in the nineteenth century outside that rather limited area. I recommend replacing "Land's End" here with "West Cornwall" (which is usefully vaguer).' **Ed.**

64 Pryce, W. (1778) *Mineralogia Cornubiensis*, Phillips, London.

65 The size of the gallon is uncertain. Barton (1971) (op. cit., ref. 34) says that a gallon of charcoal comprised 'six Winchester wine-quarts': a mysterious statement, since each size of gallon normally contained four of the corresponding quarts. The various gallons are as follows:

> Modern English gallon 4.55 litres
> Winchester gallon 4.41 litres
> Modern American gallon 3.79 litres
> (The once-familiar 'Winchester quart', in which laboratory solvents came, held 2.25 litres and was properly a half-gallon.) In working to English gallons I may have somewhat over-estimated the consumption of charcoal. I take the hundredweight at its modern value of 112 pounds, 50 kilograms or one-twentieth of a ton.

66 Rowse (1969) (op. cit., ref. 38).

67 Maclean, J. (1874) 'The tin trade of Cornwall in the reigns of Elizabeth and James, compared with that of Edward I' *Journal of the Royal Institution of Cornwall* 15 pp. 187–90.

68 Pearse, R. (1963) *The Ports and Harbours of Cornwall*, H. E. Warne, St Austell.

69 Booker, F. (1967) *Industrial Archaeology of the Tamar Valley*, David and Charles, Newton Abbot.

70 Henderson (1937).

71 Henderson (1937).

72 Henderson (1937).

73 Rackham (2003).

74 Rackham (2003) pp. 154, 164.

75 CoRO: D DV EA/24.

76 Money in the 1820s was worth about half its value in the 1650s.

77 Rackham (1976, 1990).

78 Helston Lake map: Oliver Padel says 'this eighteenth-century "Helston Lake" map (referring presumably to Loe Pool, though evidently extending to the Helford too) lacks a reference giving the location of the MS, which is a great pity.' It is unknown to him. **Ed.**

79 Oliver Rackham originally said 'the present Oak Wood already existed'. Oliver Padel says that Oliver Rackham must here mean Oak Grove (SW649258+), on the Penrose estate, north-western side of Loe Pool; so named 1888 OS 6-inch and modern maps and he doesn't know of its having ever been called Oak Wood. **Ed.**

80 Draft OS (1811: these are in the British Library on Wikipedia).

81 Oliver Padel says of the statement: 'Most of the early plantations were on the south side of the Helford River, on the Trelowarren and Penrose estates.' "There is no estate (or any other place) called Penrose on the south side of the Helford River (nor on the north side, come to that), and I think that 'Penrose' here must be a slip of the pen for 'Tremayne' SW7325, on the south side of the Helford. That seems more likely than that he meant the Penrose estate on the west side of Loe Pool, nowhere near the Helford but the only substantial Penrose estate in the area." **Ed.**

82 V[yvyan], J. S. (1976) *Trelowarren and the Vyvyan family*, Beric Tempest and Co.

83 CoRO: Tithe surveys and maps for Constantine, Wendron, Mawgan, St Martin, Manaccan, St Anthony. (I am grateful for the help of O. Padel.)

84 CoRO: TA 161.

85 Rackham (1986)b.

86 Grey squirrel: In Rackham (1986)a he says of introduced grey squirrels: "In North America the grey squirrel is regarded as harmless. In Britain it is treated as a serious pest because it damages trees, especially beech

and sycamore, by gnawing the bark. This is not always regrettable, for beech and sycamore can be pests themselves, but greys also take eggs and young birds … The most serious ecological effect of greys is probably on hazel. They pluck off the entire crop of hazelnuts in September; they may not eat them all, but those that they bury are too unripe to grow. Where nutting was an important social occasion a century ago, it is now impossible to find a single ripe nut. In grey squirrel territory I rarely see a young hazel except in the Bradfield Woods (where squirrels are persecuted) or in the gardens of friends who keep airguns. Hazel, which has shaped our civilisation since prehistoric times, is the most seriously threatened British tree except elms." The statement about hazel is controversial and many ecologists disagree, although it is likely hazel is much less prolific a coloniser than it was. My own garden has wild hazels despite having many grey squirrels. **Ed.**

87 Oliver Rackham originally wrote here: 'although I do not know of an early park at Trelowarren'. Oliver Padel says that "in fact Trelowarren is marked as having a deer-park 'emparked before 1560' on Henderson's map (*ECH* p. 158). (I do not know why he chose the date of 1560, but this date does not mean he thought it was only emparked in the sixteenth century; I think this is adequate evidence that Henderson knew of an 'early park' there, and Oliver Rackham's statement should be deleted as a slip.) Oliver Rackham refers later (under Trelowarren Wood) to a large wood-bank 'which has long served as a boundary to Trelowarren Park', so it seems he did know of this park." **Ed.**

88 Henderson (1937).

89 Rackham (1980, 2003) chapter 30.

90 The term native species excludes planted trees and shrubs (such as pines, sycamore and rhododendrons) and plants which are garden-escapes.

91 Rackham (2006) chapter 13 'Wild and planted trees'.

92 Rackham (1986)a chapter 11. These statements are based on investigation of elms by the author and the late D. E. Coombe in the 1960s and 1970s. The late-twentieth-century outbreak of Dutch Elm Disease, though it did not exterminate the elms, killed most of the big trees and made it difficult to identify the types.

93 Reported by Andrew Byfield.

94 Henderson (1935)a pp. 141–4.

95 Oliver Rackham put the words 'holm oak' here; he clearly planned a section on the tree but did not write it. Oliver Padel says: "I am confident to have seen it in the Helford area but cannot cite individual examples. It is mentioned again on page 35 and (with more detail) on page 39." **Ed.**

96 Oliver Padel says: "Edgar Thurston (1930) *British and Foreign Trees and Shrubs in Cornwall*, Cambridge University Press, (a book which Oliver Rackham doesn't seem to cite) mentions an avenue at Trelowarren, 'said to have been planted about 1837', and one tree there (whether in the avenue is not made clear) of girth 18 ft 8 in. at 3 ft from the base. In default of

anything else this information could be noted. (Incidentally it does seem odd that Oliver Rackham doesn't refer to Thurston; I suppose he was used to observing everything for himself; but one would expect then to compare one's findings with what others had previously noted.)" **Ed.**

97 Tichen, T. (2000) 'Tree gazing around Bristol: the top ten tree hybrids' *Nature in Avon* 60 pp. 55.

98 Dehnen-Schmutz, K. and Williamson, M. (2006) '*Rhododendron ponticum* in Britain and Ireland: social, economic and ecological factors in its successful invasion' *Environment and History* 12 pp. 325–50.

99 Oliver Padel says: "One might here refer to the exceptional contribution made by Cornish gentlemen in the nineteenth century to the introduction of various types of rhododendron, with (I believe) some of the oldest garden specimens growing in some Cornish gardens such as Caerhays (e.g. Thurston [1930], pp. 196–9, op. cit., ref. 96)." **Ed.**

100 Milne, R. I. and Abbott, R. J. (2000) 'Origin and evolution of invasive naturalized material of *Rhododendron ponticum* L. in the British Isles' *Molecular Ecology* 9 pp. 541–56.

101 Reported by Nigel Davies.

102 Rackham (1980, 2003) chapter 5.

103 Nature Conservancy Council: SSSI citation for Merthen Wood, 1986. (OR notes cryptically in his manuscript that this weevil was also recorded in 1932 in Gweek Wood [credit: R. T. Bannister] plus in Tremayne Creek Wood [undated and uncredited]. The Blue Notebook entry on page 30 of the South Helford River notebook from which the manuscript notes were evidently taken has no more to say, unfortunately, except that it hints at Keith Alexander of Exeter as the source of this information.) **Ed.**

104 Information from C. Preston.

105 Peterken (1981).

106 Except on the upper slopes of Merthen Wood, where exposure is great and hazel withstands it better than oak.

107 The original sentence reads: 'This has happened in the small coppiced area in this wood, which after about … years is now a thicket of pole-sized oaks.' The coppicing section on pp. 90 mentions a coppiced area in Calamansack from 1970, which is probably the area mentioned here; but the Blue Books for 1986 also mention a felled glade area about four years before with oak regrowth to 5 ft. But we do not know what year Oliver Rackham wrote this comment. **Ed.**

108 Rackham (1986)a chapter 17.

109 1308 and 1331 refs. to Henderson (1937) **Ed.**

110 Oliver Rackham originally had this reference as Rowe (1914) op. cit, ref. 25 but in fact this information is found in Vol. II not Vol. I. **Ed.**

111 *CAD* A.8646.

112 Henderson (1937).

113 Cosawes Wood CoRO: TA 72.

114 Oliver Padel says about '… on the Edgecombe Downs …' "This name is unknown to me in the vicinity of Devichoys Wood; it is not in the Tithe Apportionments of Mylor or St Gluvias parishes. It is entirely plausible, since the Edgcumbe family were landowners around here; there is a nineteenth-century village of Edgcumbe, built on former downland, 4½ miles to the south-west, and I wonder if some confusion has crept in." **Ed.**

115 Devichoys Wood CoRO: TA 161.

116 Grambla 1: Oliver Padel says: "The Lanhydrock Atlas, showing Grambla Great and Little Woods in detail, has now been published in facsimile: Holden, Herring and Padel (2010) Cornwall Editions; the map of Grambla appears on p. 168 (= II, 28 of the original atlas). The section including Grambla is in fact dated precisely to 1695 (though other parts of the Atlas have other dates or none, and are therefore *c.*1696). Rather than Oliver Rackham's original wording here ('He has found a Great and Little Wood attached to "Gramla" farm'), it would be preferable to say, 'Grambla Wood, divided into a Great and Little Wood, is shown at slightly greater extent (at the south-west corner) than on the 1888 OS 6-inch map, covering in total 59 statutory acres at that date.'" I have changed this as Oliver Padel suggests. **Ed.**

117 Grambla 2: Oliver Padel says: "I am sure that Oliver Rackham would have wished to record that the fields on the east side of the valley, under discussion in this paragraph, which were furze and croft in the nineteenth century, were already described as 'furze past[ure]' in 1695 in the Atlas, though at that date they belonged not to Grambla but to the neighbouring farm to the east, Tregoose." **Ed.**

118 Grambla 3: Oliver Padel says of the comment 'A very strong bank … not noticed on the 1841 map, divided the wood.' "It seems very likely that this is the division between Great Wood (to the south) and Little Wood (to the north), as shown on both the Lanhydrock Atlas in 1695 and on the OS 6-inch in 1888." **Ed.**

119 Grambla 4: Oliver Padel notes that, where Oliver Rackham disagrees with the evidence of the Tithe Apportionment that this (now) woodland was furze in 1841, the Lanhydrock Atlas provides strong evidence that it was so in 1695; but that may explain why the Tithe Commissioners wrongly recorded it thus in 1841, against the evidence of Oliver Rackham's observations. It seems likely that the woodland had spread here at some date after 1695, but perhaps before 1841, though not recorded so at the time. **Ed.**

120 Merthen Wood (East and West): Oliver Padel gives the reference: Henderson (1937) *Constantine* pp. 94–5, 118–20. **Ed.**

121 Oliver Padel says: "I wish I could find the reference (probably in the same book (*see* ref. 116)) for the '1570 court case'." **Ed.**

122 Oak Grove, Penrose: Oliver Padel says the reference for the thirteenth-century mentions of Penrose and Penventon is Henderson, (1935)a pp. 139–40. **Ed.**

123 *See* ref. 78 above. **Ed.**

124 Trelowarren Wood: Oliver Padel says of Oliver Rackham's original ending of the text here with: 'recorded 1011 years ago': "this was written evidently in 1988, but without a date specifically attached to the statement, it will not be comprehensible to most readers. '… recorded in the charter of AD 977' would be better." I have changed it as suggested. **Ed.**

125 Treverry Wood: At Oliver Padel's suggestion, I have expanded Oliver's original cryptic remark 'familiar to everyone who has been to the Lizard' by explaining that the reason is that the modern road southwards from Gweek to Coverack passes through it (sw7025). **Ed.**

126 Under Wood: Oliver Padel says that he thinks it is probably so named, not from containing 'underwood', but because it is situated below the farm of Kestle, to which it probably belonged. **Ed.**

127 Cornwall inventory of ancient woodland (provisional). Nature Conservancy Council (1986).

128 Evans, J. 'Coppice Woods', in Penistan, M. (1986) 'Oak in Wessex: An Account of Field Studies 1982–4' *Forestry* 59 pp. 243–58.

129 Simon Leatherdale says: "Ash forms a very minor component of the Helford River woods, but Ash dieback disease (*Hymenoscyphus fraxineus*) will be yet another man-induced change for the woods to adapt to [for a fuller account see: Oliver Rackham (2014) *The Ash Tree*, Little Toller Books]. *Dothistroma* needle blight (*Dothistroma septosporum*) may yet affect *Pinus radiata* – which could be viewed as a boon – but at present obvious signs are not evident. Of more concern are the diseases yet to show themselves in this realm – principal amongst them (at present) is *Xylella fastidiosa*, a rapacious demon with an all-too catholic appetite and not far over the horizon." **Ed.**

Index and glossary

Abies grandis **see** fir
Agrostis canina Table 4
Agrostis stolonifera Table 4
alder *Alnus glutinosa* 11, 54, Table 3, 115, 120, 125, Fig. 7.20, 126, 130, 135, 147
alder buckthorn *Frangula alnus* 74, 87, 120
Alexander, Keith 120, 170
Allium **see** garlic
Alnus **see** alder
ammonia 142
Anchonidium unguiculare 120, 138
ancient woodland: woodland that has existed continuously since before a certain date (in this book *c.*1600). 9, 11, 15, 23, Fig. 1.3, 39, 43, Fig. 3.5, 49, 56, 61, 68, 70, 74, 78, 94, 110, 111, 123, 127, 128, 135, 138, 139, 141
Andrena praecox 120
Andricus quercuscalicis 148
anemone, wood *Anemone nemorosa* 114, Fig. 7.14, 117
angelica *Angelica sylvestris* 90
Anglo-Saxons 36, 98
Aquilegia vulgaris **see** columbine
Aroundell, John 41
arsenic 22, 48, 77, 142
arum *Arum maculatum* 112
Arundell Wood 42, 46, 52, 58, 62, 64, Fig. 6.15, 102, 121, 145, Fig. AM1
ash *Fraxinus excelsior* 11, 82, Fig. 6.5, Table 3, 87, 90, 91, 97, 98, 99, 102, 105, 106, 108, 112, 115, 120, 125, 130, 132, 135, 136, 140
ash dieback 149
Athyrium **see** lady fern
Atlantic oakwoods 27

Babington leek *Allium babingtonii* 74
banks *see* woodbanks
Bannister, R. T. 170
bark 11, 53, 56
barrow 34, Fig. 3.2, 41, 112
bastard balm *Mellitis melissophyllum* 74
bats 27
beech *Fagus sylvatica* 11, 12, 16, 25, 33, 34, 56, 59, 60, 72, 73, 82, 84, 87, 97, 101, 102, 105, 111, Fig. 7.14, 117, 120, 121, 125, 126, 132, 133, 135, 136, 140, 144, 146, 147, 151, 153, 168
bell-heather *Erica cinerea* 88, Table 4, 93, 110, 116
betony *Stachys betonica* 120, 143
bilberry *Vaccinium myrtillus* 29, 88, 110, 116, 121
Binnerton 34
birch *Betula pendula* and *B. pubescens* 87, Table 4, 114, 140, 149, 150
Black Death 40
blackthorn *Prunus spinosa* 87, 98, 100
Blechnum spicant Table 4
blowing-house Fig. 3.5, 49, 50, 67, 105
bluebell *Endymion non-scriptus* (*Hyacinthoides non-scripta*) 21, 88, 89, 90, Table 4, 101, 102, 105, 107, 110, 114, Fig. 7.14, 121, 125, 126, 130, 132, 135, 136, 138, 145
Boconnoc 27, 98
Bonallack Wood 24, 28, 41, 42, 46, Table 2, 58, 60, 62, 64, 66, Fig. 4.5, 74, Fig. 5.3, 78, Fig. 6.1, 80, 84, 85, 87, 88, 89, 91, 93, Fig. 6.12, 95, Fig. 6.13, 102, 103, Fig. 7.1, Fig. 7.2, 121, 143, Fig. AM1, 165

Bonython Plantation 101
Borlase, W. 23
Bosahan Wood 24, 50, 59, 67,
  104, Fig. 7.3
bracken *Pteridium aquilinum* 10, 9, 65,
  88, 89, 90, Table 4, 96, 101, 114, 115,
  121, 132
bramble *Rubus fruticosus* 78, 88, 89, 90,
  93, 97, 102, 107, 114, 121, 125, 126,
  132, 143, 152
Bronze Age 19, 34, 48
broom *Sarothamnus scoparius* 41, 48, 93
bryophytes 10, 15, 70, 77, 101, 142, 153
Budock Vean Table 2
Bufton (and Polglase) Wood 24, 40, 43,
  Table 2, 58, 60, 67, 105, Fig. 7.4
bugle *Ajuga reptans* 90
Byfield, Dr. A. 169

Caervallack 64, 129
Calamansack Wood 24, 29, 30, 31, 33,
  41, 43, 44, 45, 46, Table 2, 53, 54, 55,
  58, 60, 61, Fig. 4.1, 62, 63, 66, 67, 79,
  Fig. 6.2, 80, 81, Fig. 6.4, Fig. 6.5, 84,
  85, 87, Fig. 6.8, 88, 89, 90, 91, 93, 96,
  Fig. 6.14, 97, 100, Fig. 7.5, Fig. 7.8, 110,
  136, 141, 145, 150, Fig. AM4, 164, 170
Calluna see heather
campion, red *Silene dioica* 90
Carex laevigata Table 4
  C. pilulifera 120
  C. remota Table 4
  C. sylvatica Table 4
Carminowe Wood 24, 40, 41, 42, 43, 59,
  61, 65, 66, 110, Fig. 7.9, 121
Carnmenellis granite 28
Castanea see chestnut
cattle 27, 55, 60
celandine, lesser *Ranunculus ficaria* Fig. 6.11
Ceratocystis fagacearum 148
Chamaenerion angustifolium Table 4
charcoal 22, 23, 48, 49, 50, 51, 52, 53,
  54, 55, Fig. 4.1, 62, 65, 66, 104, 110,
  112, 114, 121, 124, 128, 140
charters 36, 40, 48, 131, 165

Chesher, V. 8, 166
cherry *Prunus avium* 25, 108, 136
cherry laurel *Prunus laurocerasus* 130
chestnut *Castanea sativa* 25, 73, 136
chronological periods 19
Chrysosplenium see saxifrage
Cirsium palustre Table 4
clapper bridge 128
cleavers *Galium aparine* 142
clematis *Clematis vitalba* 112
cliffs 21, 28, 72, 74, 94, 95, 96, 100,
  102, 108, 128
climate change 145
clones 25, 102, 108, 132, 133
Clowance 43, Fig. 3.5, 166
coal 44, 49, 50, 51, 52
columbine *Aquilegia vulgaris* 74, 110
conifers 25, 39, 58, 59, 60, 100, 106,
  112, 115, 120, 125, 129, 131, 133, 139,
  140, 151
Conopodium see pignut
conservation: preservation from
  destructive influences, natural decay,
  or waste.
  152–4
Constantine 24, 37, 42, 46, Table 2, 53,
  64, 66, 105, 122, 124, 127, 128
Coombe, Dr D. E. 7, 36, 164, 169
copper 49, 142
coppice: (a) underwood trees which are
  cut to near ground level every few years
  and then grow again from the stool.
  (b) woodland which is managed for
  producing such underwood.
  16, 25, Fig. 1.4, 26, 39, 58, 70, 73, 78,
  79, 80, 94, 107, 108, 114, 116, 118, 124,
  125, 126, 130, 132, 135, 136, 140, 170
coppicing 29, 43, 53, 55, 60, 85, 91,
  Table 4, 93, 96, 98, 102, 111, 121, 128,
  132, 143, 152, 153
Cornish elm *Ulmus stricta* 70
Cornwall County Council 7
Cornwall Wildlife Trust 112, 144
Corylus see hazel
Cosawes Wood 39, 42, 43, Fig. 3.5, 54,
  69, 88, 111

Coswinsawsin 40, Fig. 3.5
cow-wheat *Melampyrum pratense* 88,
 98, 143
Crawle 38
croft 114, 115, 171
Crowan 43
Culdrose (airfield) 41

Dartington Series 31
Dartmoor 48, 50, 72, 152
Davies, Nigel 150, 170
deer 33, 93, 97, 143, 144, 152
deer-park 27, 44, 45, 46, 98, 143, 144, 169
Degibna Wood 99
Devichoys Wood 39, 42, 43, Fig. 3.5, 58,
 59, 74, 88, Table 4, 112, 143, 144, 171
devil's-bit scabious *Succisa pratensis* 33
disease 146
ditch 61, Fig. 4.1, 63, 114, 122, 131
Ditrichum subulatum 76
dog's mercury 90, 107, 121, 128, 131,
 132, 135
Domesday Book 36, 37, 38, 39, 40
Dothistroma septosporum 172
Drym 43, Fig. 3.5
Dryopteris aemula 120
 D. borreri 90
 D. dilatata 89, 90
 D. filix-mas 90
 D. pseudomas 89, 135
du Maurier, Daphne, 9, 21
Dumortiera hirsuta 76

earthworks 34, Fig. 3.2, 45, 61, Fig. 4.1,
 63, 64, 110, 114, 122, 131, 133, 135
earthworms 29
East Wood 62, 63, 64
elder *Sambucus nigra* 100, 132
elm 11, 25, 30, 32, 33, 44, 70, Table 3,
 Fig. 6.7, 86, 87, 90, 102, 120, 126, 127,
 132, 133, 164, 169
 Disease 101, 147, 148
 Ulmus glabra 70, 121, 130
 U. minor 70
 U. stricta 70

enchanter's nightshade *Circaea lutetiana* 90
Endymion see bluebell
Endymion (Hyacinthoides) hispanica see
 Spanish bluebell
Epilobium montanum Table 4
epiphytes 70, 78
Erica cinerea 88, Table 4, 93, 110, 116
estovers 41
Euphorbia amygdaloides 143
E. hyberna 143
eutrophication 142
Evelyn, John 72

faggots 54, 55
Fagus see beech
Falmouth 44, 56, 116
ferns 68, 89, 90, 101, 120, 125, 132, 136
fertiliser 52, 142
field systems 34
figwort *Scrophularia nodosa* 143
filmy fern *Hymenophyllum tunbridgense* 77
fir 59, 74, 115, 125, 132
fire 93
Fissidens curnowii 77
flushes 112, 121, 131, 132
Forestry Commission 141, 152
Foster, Arnold 21, 23
foxglove *Digitalis purpurea* Table 4, 93, 133
Frangula alnus see alder buckthorn
Fraxinus see ash
Frenchman's Creek 21, 22, Fig. 3.3, Fig. 6.16
fuel 23, 25, 43, 44, 48, 49, 50, 54, 56, 98
furze *Ulex europaeus* 44, 48, 58, Table 4,
 114, 115, 133, 171

Gainey, Paul 143
galls 74, 145, 148
Ganoderma adspersum 122
garlic, wild *Allium ursinum* 36, Fig. 3.3,
 90, 131, 132
Gear 38, 64, 131
Gearhills Wood 100, 131
geology 28, 30
Gillan 128
globalisation 146

golden saxifrage *Chrysosplenium oppositifolium* 21, Fig. 6.11, 121, 131, 132
gorse *see* furze
Grambla Wood 24, 34, 59, 63, 65, 66, 87, 91, 100, 112, Fig. 7.11, 115, 141, 165, 171
Gramscatho Beds 28
granite 104, 105
ground ivy *Glechoma hederacea* 142
Groyne Point 118, 120
grubbing 59, 60, 112, 114
gunpowder 54
Gunwalloe 38, 42,
Gwarth-an-Drea 58
Gweek 22, 24, 29, 33, 51, 52, 53, 66, 84, 88, 105, 112, 115, 136
Gweek Wood 24, 34, 44, 58, 59, 65, 74, 80, Fig. 6.3, 89, 91, Table 4, 93, 110, 115, Fig. 7.12, 116, Figs. 7.13 and 7.14, 117, 138, 170

Halliggye 38, 40, 58
Hatcher, John 48
hazel *Corylus avellana* 10, 11, 13, 29, 32, Fig. 3.1, 43, 55, 83, 84, Table 3, 87, 89, 90, 91, 98, 100, 101, 102, 105, 106, 108, 111, 112, 114, 115, 120, 121, 122, 124, 126, 128, 130, 132, 135, 136
heath 10, 22, 25, 31, 45, 84, 98, 146, 151
heather *Calluna vulgaris* 27, 29, 30, 78, 88, Fig. 6.9, Table 4, 93, 96, 102, 110, 116, 121, 126, 143
Hedera see ivy
Helston 37, 48, 50, 110, 123
Henderson, Charles 8, 42, 55, 59, 66, 121, 164, 165, 166, 168, 170, 171, 172
Highweek Series 31
hillforts 34, 63, 165
Holcus lanatus Table 4
 H. mollis 110
holloways 63, 64, 65, 108, 118, 121, 133
holly *Ilex aquifolium* 10, 11, 21, 29, 83, 84, Table 3, Fig. 6.6, 89, 96, 97, 99, 100, 102, 107, 108, 111, 112, 114, 115, 120, 121, 122, 123, 126, 128, 135, 136, 140, 143, 146, 147, 149, 150

holm oak *Quercus ilex* 87, 97, 146, 151, 169
Holocene 146
honey fungus *Armillaria* 149
honeysuckle *Lonicera periclymenum* 89, 110
Hookeria lucens Fig. 5.5, 77, 105, 120
humus 29, 30
Hydrangea macrophylla 145
Hymenophyllum tunbridgense 77
Hymenoscyphus fraxineus 172
Hypericum perfoliatum Table 4, 93, 143

Ice Age 21, 28, 32, 146
Ilex see holly
invasive species 144
iron 51
Iron Age 19, 34, 64, 131
Isle of Wight 144
ivy *Hedera helix* 88, 89, 114, 132

jay 97
jellyfish 9

Kelliancrek (*Kelly-an-crek*) 41, 42, 43
Kerrier 37, 44, 51, 52, 85
Knopper gall Fig. 8.3, 149

lady fern *Athyrium filix-femina* 90
Lathyrus montanus 120
Leatherdale, S. 165, 172
leats 67, 105, 112, 131,
Leland, John 44
Lemon (family) 111, 112
Leptura orulenta (longhorn beetle) 120
lichens 10, 27, 77, 78, 132, 136, 142, 152, 153
lignotubers Fig. 6.12, 94
Limax cinereoniger (slug) 120
lime *Tilia cordata* 70, Fig. 5.2, 72, 87, 95, 130
limekilns 45, Fig. 3.5, 52, Fig. 3.6, 66, 67
Lizard (Peninsula) 28, 31, 32, 33, 34, 36, 38, 43, 48, 68, 69, 74, 136, 142
Lobaria pulmonaria 143
Loe Pool 56, 99, 168
loess 28, 29, 30

Lonicera see honeysuckle
Lucombe, William 73
Luzula pilosa Table 4
Luzula sylvatica see woodrush
lyncenin 36

marble gall *Andricus kollari* 148, 149
Mawgan 38, 50, 116
Megalithic 112
Melittis melissophyllum see bastard balm
Mellangoose 40
Meneage 30, 31, Fig. 3.5, 100
 Crush Zone 28
Merthen Hole 22, 66, 118, 121
Merthen Wood Fig. 1.2, 24, 25, 30, 34,
 41, 42, 43, 44, 45, 46, Table 2, 52, 53,
 54, 55, 56, 58, 59, 60, 62, 63, 64, Fig.
 4.3, 66, 68, 69, 70, 74, 79, Fig. 6.2, 81,
 82, 84, 85, 87, 88, Fig. 6.9, 90, Fig. 6.13,
 97, 98, Fig. 7.1, 110, 118–22 Fig. 7.15,
 Fig. 7.16, Fig. 7.17, 138, Fig. 8.1, 141,
 143, Fig. 8.4, 154, Fig. AM2, Fig. AM3,
 170, 171
Mesolithic 19, 22, 143
Microsphaera alphitoides see Oak mildew
Middle Ages: (in this book) 1066 to 1536.
 19, 23, 34, 40, 42, 50, 144
mill 41, 64, 105, 127, 140
montbretia 145
mor 29
mosses 76, 78, 120, 132, 136, 152
mull 29, 30, 31
Mylor 38, 112, 171

Nancenoy 42
Nance Wood 72
National Trust 123, 128, 132, 141,
 152, 153
Nature Conservancy Council 138, 139
Neolithic 19, 27, 33, 34, 42
nettle *Urtica dioica* 90, 121, 132, 142
nightingale 93
Nomada ferruginata (parasite of bee) 120

oak 32, 55, 56, 66, 68, 69, 73, Fig. 6.3,
 84, 85, Fig. 6.6, Fig. 6.9, 91, 93, Fig. 6.12,
 96, Fig. 6.14, 100, 101, 105, Fig. 7.6,
 114, 118, 120, 146, 147
Quercus cerris see Turkey oak
Q. petraea 25, 27, 68–9, Fig. 5.1, 78, Fig. 6.1
Q. robur 27, 68, 69, 110, 112, 125
Oak Grove 56, 84, 99, 123, Fig. 7.18,
 168, 172
Oak mildew *Microsphaera alphitoides* Fig.
 6.17, 101, 146, 153
Oak Wilt *Ceratocystis fagacearum* 147, 148
oakwoods 10, 33, 84, Table 3, 89, 102,
 115, Fig. 7.17, 127, 135, 139, 143, 144,
 149, 150, 151
Oenanthe crocata 91, 121, 132, 135
orpine *Sedum telephium* 74, Fig. 5.4, 131
Oudemansiella mucida 122
Padel, Oliver 113, 164, 165, 166, 167,
 168, 169, 170, 171, 172
pannage 43
park pale 64
peat 48, 49, 50, 132
pedunculate oak *Quercus robur* 27, 68,
 110, 112, 125
Penbothidnow Table 2
Pencoose 40
Pencoys 40
Pengelly 40
Penrose Wood 42, Fig. 3.5, 56, 84
Penryn 43, 44, Fig. 3.5, 112
Penventon Wood 42, 123
Penwith 38, 40, 44, 51,
 perambulations 36
pests 146
Peterken, George 85, 164, 170
phenology 145, 146
*Phytophthora infestans, alni, kernoviae,
ramorum* 147
pignut 96
pill: an inlet or harbour off a river or
 creek, often tidal.
 21, 22, 44, 64, 65, 67, 102, 107,
 108, Fig. 7.15, 118, 120, 122
pine 111, 122

Pinus maritima 101
Pinus radiata 60, 140, 153, 172
plantation: closely-spaced stand of trees, other than an orchard, formed by sowing or planting the trees.
23, 25, 27, 39, 56, 58, 59, 69, 82, 99, 100, 101, 105, 108, 110, 112, 122, 130, 131, 132, 136, 140, 141, 150, 151, 153, 154
podzolisation 29, 31
poisoning 95, 125, 144
Polglase Wood **see** Bufton Wood
pollard: tree which is cut at 8–12 ft (2.5–3 m) above ground-level and allowed to grow again from the bolling to produce successive crops of wood.
Fig. 1.4, 27, 73, 84, 99, 123
pollen 32, 33, 72
pollution 142, 143
Polwartha Table 2, 124
Polwheveral Wood 24, Table 2, 59, 66, 124–5, Fig. 7.19
polypody fern *Polypodium vulgare* 21, 70, 78, 106, Fig. 7.6, 136
Polystichum setiferum 74
Ponsanooth 111
Ponsaverrion Table 2
Porthnavas Creek 23, 44, 58, 60, Fig. 4.1, 100
Portreath Wood 39
powder mill 111, 112
Preston, Dr. C. 170
primrose *Primula vulgaris* 90, Fig. 6.11, 101

quarry Fig. 3.6, Fig. 4.5, 104, 105, 136
quay 52, 64, 66–7, Fig. 4.4, 102, 120, 121, Fig. 7.28, 134, 135
Quercus **see** oak

rabbits 73, 144
ramsons **see** garlic
Ranunculus repens Table 4
ravines 21, 42, 58, 62, 79, 102, 106, 107, 108, Fig. 7.7, 114, 115, 118, 120, 121, 131, 136, 142, 144, 152, 153

recent woodland 11, 15, 23, 27, 100, 112, 135, 138
red campion *Silene dioica* 90, Table 4, 133
re-planting 25, 59, 68, 82, 116, 126, 129, 131, 132, 138, 139, 141
Reskymmer Wood **see** Roskymmer Wood
Restronguet Wood 43, 44, Fig. 3.5
Rhamnus **see** buckthorn
Rhododendron catawbiense 73
Rhododendron ponticum 73, 87, Table 4, 112, 140, 144, 147, 151, 170
Roman 19, 34, Fig. 3.2, 64, 73, Fig. 7.16
rooks 97
Roskymmer (Reskymmer) Wood Fig. 3.1, 40, 41, Fig. 3.5, 50, 53, 60, 61, 72, 125–6, Fig. 7.20, Fig. 7.21, 139
rounds 34, 35, 60, 63, 64, 112, 128, 129, 131, 133
rowan *Sorbus aucuparia* 84, 102, 120, 126
royal fern *Osmunda regalis* 74, 90, 101, 114, 120, 128
Rubus fruticosus Table 4
Rumex acetosella Table 4

St Austell 49
St Gluvias 112, 171
Salix **see** sallow
sallow *Salix caprea* 87, 100, 101, 106, 128, 130
salt 81, 95
sanicle *Sanicula europaea* 110
Sannan Series 31
Sarothamnus scoparius **see** broom
savanna: trees scattered in grassland or other non-shade-bearing vegetation, equivalent to uncompartmented forms of wood-pasture.
27, 42, 145
saw-wort *Serratula tinctoria* 143
saxifrage *Chrysosplenium oppositifolium* **see** golden saxifrage
Scots pine *Pinus sylvestris* 101
seaweed 21, 45, 96
Secomb Wollas Table 2
secondary woodland: woodland now on sites which have formerly

been farmland, moorland, plotland, plantation, wood-pasture, etc. 25, 56, 58, 60, Fig. 6.16, 105, 122, 123
Sedum telephium see orpine
Senecio erucifolius Table 4
Serrion ferruginatum 120
service (wild) *Sorbus torminalis* 25, 74, Fig. 5.3, 84, 94, 102, 108, 120
sessile oak *Quercus petraea* 27, 68–9, Fig. 5.1, 78, Fig. 6.1, Table 3
shade 143
sheep 27, 55
sheep's sorrel *Rumex acetosella* Table 4, 93
shredding Fig. 1.4, 26, 54
Site of Special Scientific Interest 139, 141
Skewys, John 52
skull cap *Scutellaria minor* 74
small-leaved lime *Tilia cordata* 32
soil 28, 29, 30, 31, 32, 33, 68, 85, 87, 89, 91, 93, 97, 110, 111, 112, 116, 127, 132, 138, 143, 164
Solomon's seal *Polygonatum multiflorum* 74, 131
Sonchus oleraceus Table 4
Sorbus see rowan and service
Spanish bluebell *Endymion (Hyacinthoides) hispanica* 145
springs 30, Table 3, 87, 91, 132, 135, 136
squirrel
grey 60, 73, 144, 168, 169
red 32
Stachys betonica see betony
standard: a woodland or hedgerow tree suitable for timber. 25, 127
standing-stone 34, Fig. 3.2
stools Fig. 1.4, 70, 72, 73, Fig. 6.1, 80, 81, 93, 94, 95, 96, 99, 100, 105, 107, 108, 111, 114, 116, 118, 120, 121, 125, 127, 128, 135, 136, 140, 149,
strawberry 90, 136
streams 31, 36, 50, 63, 105, 110, 114, 115, 121, 130, 131
Sudden Oak Death 147
sulphur dioxide 142

sycamore *Acer pseudoplatanus* 59, 60, 72, 73, 82, 97, 98, 100, 102, 105, 111, 120, 122, 125, 126, 132, 133, 136, 144, 147, 151, 169
tanning 53
Tehidy 39
Teloschistes flavicans Fig. 8.2, 143
threats 140
Three Lords Wood 59
thrift 96
Tilia see lime
timber: trunks of trees, of more than a certain diameter, suitable for making beams or sawing into planks (normally oak unless otherwise stated). 25, 27, 41, 43, 44, 51, 53, 59, 60, 73, 78, 79, Fig. 6.2, 95, 108, 114, 121, 125, 126, 132, 141
timberwood 79, 80, 102, 107, 108, 112, 114, 116, 120, 128, 152
tin 21, 22, 23, 48, 49, 50, 51, 54, 77, 115
Tolvan 59
Tolvan-Wartha Wood 24, Table 2, 127–8, Fig 7.22
Tolvan-Wollas (Bufton) Wood 24, 40, Table 2, 61, 80, 84, 85, 89, 105, Fig. 7.4
Trebe Wartha Table 2
tree communities Fig 6.5, 78, 84, 88, Fig. 7.27
Tree Preservation Order 141
Tregithey Wood 24, 60, 65, 66, 80, 89, Fig. 6.1, 100, 128–9, Fig. 7.23
Tregoose 40, 171
Trelowarren Mills Wood 24, 31, 59, 61, 67, 68, 76, 82, 91, 131–2, 141, 154
Trelowarren Wood 24, 30, 31, 36, 38, 40, 56, 59, 63, 64, 68, 70, Fig. 5.2, 74, 78, 87, 90, 91, 129–31, Fig. 7.24, Fig. 7.25, 139, 140, 169, 172
Tremayne Great Wood 24, 29, 30, 31, 56, 61, 63, 64, 69, 70, 73, 78, 80, 84, 85, Fig. 6.7, 87, 90, Fig. 6.11, Table 4, 93, 97, 101, 132–3, Fig. 7.26, Fig. 7.27, Fig. 7.28, 138, 139, 141, 152, 153, Fig. AM5

Tremayne Little Wood 24, 30, 31, 59, 61, Fig. 4.2, 65, 67, 68, 82, 133–5, Fig. 7.26, 138, 141, 153, Fig. AM5
Trenarth Table 2
Trengilly Table 2
Tresaher Vean Table 2
Trethewey 36
Treverry Wood 24, 59, Fig. 6.6, 91, Table 4, 93, 96, 135–6, Fig. 7.29, 172
Treviades Table 2
Truthall 38, 40
Tucoyse 38, 40, 46, Table 2, 53, 127
Turkey Oak *Quercus cerris* 59, 73, 87, 125, 144, 146, 148, 149
Tutsan *Hypericum androsaemum* 74, 111

Ulex see furze
Ulmus see elm
Under Wood 136–7, Fig. 7.30, 172
underwood: wood (whether growing or cut) consisting of coppice poles, young suckers, or (less often) pollard poles. 25, 41, 43, 51, 53, 55, 78, 80, Fig. 6.2, 114, 126, 131
urbanisation 23, 60
Urtica see nettle

variegated archangel *see* yellow archangel
vegetation 78
Vellan Tremayne 64, 67, 74, 95, 133
Vera, Frans 33, 164
Veronica montana see wood speedwell
violet Fig. 6.11
Vyvyan 40, 56, 61, 72, 168
wall 61, 63, 101, 105, 110, 112, 114, 121, 131, 135, 136

watermill 25, 131
water wheel 67
weeding 55
Wendron 105, 114
Wheal Fire 105
wild garlic *see* garlic
wild madder *Rubia peregrine* 96
wild service *see* service
wildwood: prehistoric forest of the pre-Neolithic period [supposedly] unaffected by organised human activities. 23, 27, 32, 33, 34, 70, 72, 84, 87
windblow 153
Winnington 37, Fig. 3.4, 42, 43
wood anemone *see* anemone, wood
woodbank: boundary bank surrounding (or subdividing) a wood. 61, Fig. 4.1, Fig. 4.2, 63, 64, 70, 105, 107, 110, 114, 121, 122, 126, 128, 131, 133, 136, 140, 169
woodcock 60
woodmanship 42
wood-pasture: tree-land on which farm animals or deer are systematically grazed. 27, 42, 56, 68, 84, Fig. 6.15, 98, 99, 145
woodrush *Luzula sylvatica* 89, Fig. 6.10, Table 4, 93, 107, 116, 120, 128
wood sage *Teucrium scorodonia* 110
wood sorrel *Oxalis acetosella* 70, 131
wood spurge *Euphorbia amygdaloides* 88

Xyllela fastidiosa 172

yellow archangel *Lamiastrum galeobdolon ssp. montanum* 76, *ssp. argentatum* 76

Little Toller Books

We publish old and new writing attuned to nature and the landscape, working with a wide range of the very best writers and artists. If you have enjoyed this book, you will also like exploring our other titles.

Anthology and Biography
ARBOREAL: WOODLAND WORDS *Adrian Cooper*
CORNERSTONES: SUBTERRANEAN WRITING *Mark Smalley*
MY HOME IS THE SKY: THE LIFE OF J. A. BAKER *Hetty Saunders*

Field Notes
DEER ISLAND *Neil Ansell*
ORISON FOR A CURLEW *Horatio Clare*
SOMETHING OF HIS ART: WALKING WITH J. S. BACH *Horatio Clare*
THE TREE *John Fowles*
LOVE, MADNESS, FISHING *Dexter Petley*
WATER AND SKY *Neil Sentance*
THE ANCIENT WOODS OF SOUTH-EAST WALES *Oliver Rackham*
THE ANCIENT WOODS OF THE HELFORD RIVER *Oliver Rackham*

New Nature Monographs
HERBACEOUS *Paul Evans*
ON SILBURY HILL *Adam Thorpe*
THE ASH TREE *Oliver Rackham*
MERMAIDS *Sophia Kingshill*
BLACK APPLES OF GOWER *Iain Sinclair*
BEYOND THE FELL WALL *Richard Skelton*
LIMESTONE COUNTRY *Fiona Sampson*
HAVERGEY *John Burnside*
SNOW *Marcus Sedgwick*
LANDFILL *Tim Dee*
SPIRITS OF PLACE *Sara Maitland*

Nature Classics Library
THROUGH THE WOODS *H. E. Bates*
MEN AND THE FIELDS *Adrian Bell*
THE MIRROR OF THE SEA *Joseph Conrad*
ISLAND YEARS, ISLAND FARM *Frank Fraser Darling*
THE MAKING OF THE ENGLISH LANDSCAPE *W. G. Hoskins*
FOUR HEDGES *Clare Leighton*
DREAM ISLAND *R. M. Lockley*
THE UNOFFICIAL COUNTRYSIDE *Richard Mabey*
RING OF BRIGHT WATER *Gavin Maxwell*
IN PURSUIT OF SPRING *Edward Thomas*
THE NATURAL HISTORY OF SELBORNE *Gilbert White*

LITTLE TOLLER BOOKS
Lower Dairy, Toller Fratrum, Dorset DT2 oEL
w. littletoller.co.uk   E. books@littletoller.co.uk